Measuring Monarchy

MEASURING MONARCHY

THE MOST OVERRATED AND UNDERRATED BRITISH KINGS AND QUEENS

TIM HAMES

For Julia, Edward, Tom and George

Jacket illustrations: Antique crown (ilbusca/iStock); measuring tape (mecalehai/iStock); William of Normandy, as illustrated in the Bayeuz Tapestery (Myrabella/Wikimedia Commons); Elizabeth I, a 1575 painting by Johannes Corvus (Gwengoat/iStock); Queen Victoria (*London Illustrated News*).

Alexander Pope quote from *The impertinent: or a visit to the court. A satyr. By an eminent hand*, courtesy of University of Michigan Library Digital Collections https://name.umdl.umich.edu/004809270.0001.000.

First published 2025

The History Press
97 St George's Place, Cheltenham,
Gloucestershire, GL50 3QB
www.thehistorypress.co.uk

© Tim Hames, 2025

The right of Tim Hames to be identified as the Author of this work has been asserted in accordance with the Copyright, Designs and Patents Act 1988.

All rights reserved. No part of this book may be reprinted or reproduced or utilised in any form or by any electronic, mechanical or other means, now known or hereafter invented, including photocopying and recording, or in any information storage or retrieval system, without the permission in writing from the Publishers.

British Library Cataloguing in Publication Data.
A catalogue record for this book is available from the British Library.

ISBN 978 1 80399 894 7

Typesetting and origination by The History Press
Printed and bound in Great Britain by TJ Books, Padstow, Cornwall.

The History Press proudly supports

Trees for Life

www.treesforlife.org.uk

EU Authorised Representative: Easy Access System Europe
Mustamäe tee 50, 10621 Tallinn, Estonia
gpst.request@easproject.com

Contents

Introduction	7
William I (1066–87) OVERRATED	19
Stephen (1135–54) UNDERRATED	33
Henry II (1154–89) UNDERRATED	47
Richard I (1189–99) OVERRATED	61
Edward III (1327–77) UNDERRATED	75
Henry V (1413–22) OVERRATED	89
Henry VII (1485–1509) UNDERRATED	103
Henry VIII (1509–47) OVERRATED	117

Elizabeth I (1558–1603)   131
    OVERRATED

William III (1689–1702)   145
    OVERRATED

Anne (1702–14)   159
    UNDERRATED

William IV (1830–37)   175
    UNDERRATED

Victoria (1837–1901)   189
    OVERRATED

Edward VII (1901–10)   205
    UNDERRATED

Postscript: Elizabeth II (1952–2022)   219

Conclusions on Crowns   237

Further Reading   253

Introduction

This book, appropriately for the English monarchy perhaps, has something of a history to it. It started life in a small way as a response to an initiative of others. In the Christmas/New Year break of 2001/02, in anticipation of Queen Elizabeth's Golden Jubilee which would occur shortly after, the *Today* programme on BBC Radio Four decided to run a poll among its listeners as to who was the 'best' monarch ever, with a shortlist of Alfred the Great, Henry VIII, Elizabeth I, Victoria (who would emerge as the ultimate victor in this contest) and Elizabeth II. It attracted a degree of attention.

I was the Chief Leader Writer and Comment Editor of *The Times* back then and wrote a weekly column in that newspaper. My fare normally consisted of domestic or international politics, but in this fallow period between the Christmas turkey and the New Year's Eve champagne I was looking to write about something different. I offered a critique (published on 28 December 2001) of the *Today* survey because it confused fame (or even notoriety) with success, had no objective criteria for how such an assessment should be made and the five selected names excluded at least one whom I felt firmly should be there instead (Henry VII). It was an enjoyable piece to write, and it stirred up some interest among the readers. For more than two decades after that, it remained the germ of an idea for a much longer argument, one that I only turned to again in the early months of 2024.

The study of leadership, especially in the context of business and management, has become quite an industry. There are literally hundreds, quite possibly thousands, of tomes that have been published which claim to be able to separate the qualities of those who have proved highly effective leaders from others who have been either relatively inconsequential while at the helm, or outright failures.

When it comes to both monarchy and political leadership more broadly, there seems to be far less interest in what makes for an exceptional figure. There are, of course, many accounts of individuals, be they kings or queens in many countries, presidents or prime ministers, dictators or tyrants, which ask searching questions of their subject matter. There is no shortage of personality analysis.

Much the same, it will be contended here, can be said about the treatment of the monarchy in the United Kingdom. Enormous attention is devoted to character traits with the consequence that it becomes far harder to make comparisons between those who have sat on the throne than it really should be. Is Alfred the Great to be understood better because 'he burnt the cakes' or Henry VIII to be placed on some peculiar pedestal because he had six wives, or what made Queen Victoria gain the reputation that she was not amused? All of this seems to be a doubtful basis on which to look at kings or queens on their own terms, never mind seek to create a framework in which they can be compared to one another, and a reasonable judgement of their relative merits be realised. What is about to be attempted here – measuring monarchy – demands a completely different mindset.

How Can You Measure Monarchy?

There are, of course, constraints on comparison which make any such study incomplete or imperfect.

Introduction

The first lies in what is and is not included. This book is essentially about English monarchs, until the point where James I unites the Crowns of the two countries in 1603, to be followed a century later by the formal amalgamation of England and Scotland through the Act of Union (1707). This places an array of very interesting historical figures from Macbeth through William the Lion (a king totally unknown to the English, despite having reigned north of the border for almost fifty years) to Robert the Bruce out of scope. This is a decision taken not out of nationalism but because the management of the monarchy in England and Scotland would have been very different for most of the admittedly sizeable time between the Norman Conquest and 1603 or 1707. A more informed person than I might chance their arm in another book at measuring the Scottish monarchies over the centuries.

The second is that we are dealing with an extremely lengthy stretch of history during which the expectations of monarchy have changed enormously. William the Conqueror and Charles III (only one of whom is placed under the microscope in these pages) are hardly chips off the same block. In the earlier part of the history examined, the conduct of war on the battlefield itself was a crucial element in the reputation of those who wore the crown. As time moved on, a monarch was expected to be the master of domestic policy, relations with the established Church and foreign affairs, but it was not assumed that they would don a suit of armour at short notice themselves.

This book is not, though, an endeavour which aspires to construct some sort of league table in which every monarch who fits in the frame of England to 1603 and England and Scotland from that date is listed. The aim instead is to establish some general but enduring rules for deciding on relative merit, then to offer a series of case studies of who appear to be underrated and overrated respectively, and then to draw some threads together in concluding what it is that the underrated have in common.

The task is not as taxing as it might seem to be anyway. Comparing William I (the Conqueror) (1066–87) with Stephen (1135–54) is not an impossible aim as Norman England (once the invaders had become a fully occupying force) did not change that dramatically between the dates concerned. Henry II (1154–89) was succeeded by Richard I or Lionheart (1189–99). It is not that hard to draw a comparison between Edward III (1327–77) and Henry V (1413–22), where there is not a chasm in their timespans. The monarchs Henry VII (1485–1509), Henry VIII (1509–47) and Elizabeth I (1558–1603) are Tudor family. William III (1689–1702) is followed by Anne (1702–14). William IV (1830–37), Victoria (1837–1901) and Edward VII (1901–10) come after one another. These fourteen kings and queens comprise those who are to be awarded either an 'underrated' or an 'overrated' designation.

The Ratings

The use of terms like 'underrated' and 'overrated' only makes sense if there is some degree of consensus about those who are either 'accurately rated' or 'fairly rated'. To a perhaps rather surprising extent, this writer believes that most historical observers would not have that much difficulty determining who should be rated 'good', 'average', 'poor', 'terrible' or 'not rateable'.

THE GOOD
The 'good' (excluding, as will be the case uniformly here, the fourteen monarchs scheduled for a closer inspection) include Henry I, Edward I, Henry IV (a slightly edgy choice, some would assert) and (on balance) Edward IV. As will be outlined at the end of this book, Elizabeth II may well fit here too.

The Average
The 'average' (in chronological order) would include William II, James I (possibly at the top of this division), Charles II, George II (perhaps close to the relegation zone), George V and George VI.

The Poor
The 'poor' (in order of their reign) contains John, Henry III, Mary Tudor, George I (although it is a judgement call between the first two Hanoverians as to who is the less appealing), George III (it was not his fault that he was consumed by insanity, but a device should have been found for abdication in these conditions) and George IV. They tainted the monarchy to a degree but were not overthrown.

The Terrible
The 'terrible' were actually thrown out. They number Edward II (removed by his wife, her lover and his own heir), Richard II (deposed by Henry IV), Henry VI (ejected by Edward IV), Richard III (although he has his defenders, who would not be pleased to see him placed in this company), Charles I (not a smart king even if the royalists were 'wrong but romantic') and his son James II (forced to flee).

The Remainder
There is then a small set of kings and queens who for diverse reasons are hard to categorise at all. Edward V disappeared from the Tower of London, assumed murdered as a child. Edward VI was a boy king under the control of first the Duke of Somerset, then the Duke of Northumberland. Mary II, in theory the joint monarch with her husband William III, was plainly the inferior party in that contract and died after just over five years on the throne. Edward VIII abdicated within a year so that he could marry Wallis Simpson (although there is a plausible lobby that would mark him

down as 'terrible' for that decision and his liaisons with Adolf Hitler and the Nazis). Charles III is too new to judge.

The Evaluation Here

The central premise of this book is that a series of monarchs whom many would automatically list as 'good', even 'great', should not have that status and that a series of other figures (some of whom are well known but have been burdened by an unfair assessment) should be elevated from an 'average' ranking, which most of them would conventionally have, and now be evaluated as 'good' rulers.

There is, nonetheless, one final constraint that should be conceded at the outset of the operation. It is surely unavoidable even if strenuous efforts are made to minimise it. It cannot be obliterated.

It is subjectivity. Even if there were to be a universal consensus that the five measures which are about to be outlined are indeed the ideal means by which monarchs should be evaluated (and it would be a miracle on the scale of the loaves and the fishes if that were to come to pass), then that still leaves an immense amount to disagree about in how those measures should be utilised. At the extremes, there are occasions where it is absolutely clear whether a monarch did or did not leave the public finances in a better or worse state than they inherited, or engaged in wars which either did or did not make England, or England and Scotland, a bigger player on the European (later global) stage and whether the succession which would follow their deaths would be smooth or contested.

There are other instances, though, when it is not as clear-cut how to validate a verdict. There may be a case that the strength or weakness of the coffers was not a direct reflection on the monarch of the day, or that their options in the exercise of foreign policy were either wider or narrower, or that the succession question arose in circumstances which it was unreasonable for them to have expected.

Introduction

There will doubtless be observers of certain figures, whom I believe can be dispassionately assigned as 'underrated' or 'overrated', who will examine the same acts or events in history and come to an entirely different conclusion as to how they should be interpreted. Subjectivity is destined never to be removed from historical deliberation altogether. In truth, it is the blood flowing in its veins.

Without an element of structure, and one which is not too open-ended or ambiguous, the aspiration to measure monarchy is lost before it has even started in earnest. We need some rules, or we have little chance of reaching findings, even if they will still prompt dissent thereafter. What are set out now are the five measures by which, it will be asserted here, we can examine the record of monarchs not only in terms of what their contemporaries might have thought, but more widely.

Metrics for Monarchy

The first of these metrics is the standing of the monarch in relation to other institutions of the state (such as the nobility, Parliament and the Church, with the balance across them evolving over time).

Professional reputation is in many regards the spine of leadership. It is not a formal requirement for legitimacy, but there is no doubt that it can render stronger a monarch whose initial claim to the throne was based on a bloodline that was more than capable of dispute, and, in equal spirit, it can lead a monarch whose standing at the time they acquired the Crown was solid into disrepute if others who have influence over the direction of the country come to lose confidence in their abilities. In the most dire of conditions, a monarch whose share price among the very small number of stakeholders who count sinks to an unacceptable low will find themselves heading for the exit by one means or another, as in different ways was true for Edward II (deposed and then disposed of), Richard II (ditto), Henry III (whose grip on his title was frequently threatened), Henry VI (forced out between 1461 and 1470, briefly restored as a titular ruler from 1470 to 1471, before returning to the Tower of London once more), Richard III (killed in battle), Charles I (through the mechanism of a civil war and the indignity of capture, execution and displacement by an entirely new constitutional order) and his son James II (enforced abdication, although religion mattered here more than perceived ineptitude).

The need to command the respect of others within the national elite extends to others whose fate was not as spectacular in their demise. Richard III was held responsible for the death of the boy king Edward V, which hardly assisted in his own acceptability as king to others. George III was in the thrall of madness but there was no mechanism for removing him into retirement. Edward VIII was not mad but might have had more chance of engineering a compromise over his marriage had his behaviour not convinced leading Conservative and Labour figures alike that abdication was the least bad option.

The second is the **popular standing of the monarch with broader public opinion** in so far as this can be divined and in so far as it was important to their authority on the throne. This is admittedly much easier to come to an opinion about in later times than earlier ones. Public sentiment did not count for much under the Plantagenets or explain the ebb and flow of what would come to be known as the War of the Roses. It did, however, probably aid Henry IV's cause that he was the first monarch since the Norman Conquest to have English as his native tongue. The Duke of Northumberland's scheme to ensure that Lady Jane Grey came after the sickly Edward VI fell apart because of a mass instinct that Mary Tudor held the legitimacy card in proceedings (although if there had been a half-viable male contender for the Tudor Crown, they might have had a shot at it). In more recent times, the consistent and intense unpopularity of George IV can hardly have been an asset to him. This was a king whose obituary in *The Times* opened with the sentence, 'There never was an individual less regretted by his fellow creatures than this deceased King' and did not improve much thereafter.[1]

A mastery of the popular touch became vital from the early twentieth century onwards. Sympathy towards George VI allowed him to overcome concerns at the pinnacle of the Establishment as to whether he was physically capable of fulfilling his functions (a fear which his own wife and consort may have shared) and enabled him to escape what turned out to be the horror show of a crass miscalculation in inviting Neville Chamberlain to share the balcony of Buckingham Palace in the immediate aftermath of the Munich Agreement, which within months would prove a failure. The extraordinary scenes after the death of Diana, Princess of Wales led to open deliberation as to whether her ex-husband had become too tarnished to be king once Elizabeth II had passed on. This dimension is today arguably the most important aspect in deciding the survival of the monarchy.

The third component is the skill or not of a monarch in their **handling of the public finances.** This was of sizeable importance when the monarch was the active de facto chief executive of the country. No one in the twenty-first century, by contrast, would hold the House of Windsor to account for the votes of the Monetary Policy Committee of the Bank of England or the musings of the Office for Budget Responsibility, but in a previous era fiscal competence would have been essential. Those who had to resort to the sale of land and titles within the nobility would be more likely to make enemies than friends, while any additional taxation on the peasant class was rarely a winning strategy either. Monarchs who were either excessive with the

---

1   *The Times*, 15 July 1830.

extravagance at their own court or inclined to fight expensive wars where victory brought few spoils and defeat meant more financial sacrifice were not rated highly by their contemporaries (or many historians for that matter). Those who could deliver prosperity were likely to find that they had more latitude in their other dealings as the monarch.

The fourth element is the **conduct of foreign policy**, be that in matters of war or in diplomacy. The balance between the two is seminal to the standing of those who occupied the throne. Before 1066, this meant the ability to handle what we would now call Denmark, Norway and Sweden. For almost 500 years after that, England was a force of its own in France (and, indeed, France in England as the heirs to William the Conqueror remained very French indeed for centuries afterwards). It fell to the Tudors to deal with the sudden rise of Spain, although that country declined not long after. Even after the Restoration and the 'Glorious Revolution' which had demonstrated the command of Parliament, the monarch was allowed the dominant role in foreign policy and national security, with France restored as the primary concern at court and in Westminster. Matters became more awkward when the House of Hanover (briefly Saxe-Coburg-Gotha) found itself in apposition to Germany, even if by the twentieth century this was largely symbolic with the prime minister the commander-in-chef to all intents and purposes. Diplomacy still remains within the orbit of the monarchy, as was illustrated by Elizabeth II's dogged support for the Commonwealth as an organisation of meaning and the extent to which Charles III can highlight his own not inconsiderable international environmental role. Monarchs have varied hugely in their ability to 'make the weather' with diplomatic engagement.

The final aspect is among the most sensitive (at times, the most unspeakable subject in public), namely **succession**. This is not only about whether a monarch has a direct heir – an adult child (very much ideally) of his or her own to pass the throne on to – although this has usually proved more stable than more distant bloodlines, but also about the character of their relationship and their willingness to concede their own mortality and actively educate and train that heir in statecraft.

There have been a host of examples of catastrophic human relationships among monarchs. Edward I had all but given up on Edward II long before the transfer of power happened. Mary was deeply reluctant to signal that her younger sister, Elizabeth, would be her rightful successor as she suspected (correctly) that the renewed authority of the Bishop of Rome which she had engineered would be in peril. Probably the most toxic dynamic of the lot (although competition for this is hot) is that between George I and George II. Well before he had become King of England and Scotland, George I had dispensed of his wife Sophia Dorothea. Although his fondness for mistresses was legendary, the then aspiring Elector of Hanover was incensed by Sophia Dorothea's liaison with a Swedish count, Philip Christoph von Königsmarck, who was mysteriously murdered in 1694 and in a gruesome fashion (in one account, hacked to pieces on the direct order of the enraged husband before being thrown into a river).

Immediately following this scandalous event, George arranged for his divorce from Sophia Dorothea on the basis that she had abandoned him, and he had her incarcerated in Ahlden House where she was to stay for more than thirty years before she died. The future George II had rather more loyalty to his mother than to his father and they were thus barely on speaking terms.

Succession does not have to be as sensational as that to be a vital test of monarchical aptitude. If it is not addressed, then it can haunt an entire reign with courtiers endlessly engaged in whispers as to what would happen if the incumbent monarch were to meet with an unfortunately timed demise.

These five factors – personal standing with other institutions of the national body politic, public popularity (for later figures at any rate), financial aptitude, foreign and diplomatic policy, and the preparations for succession – are as compelling a collection of criteria for assessing the merit of a monarch across the ages as any other yardsticks might prove to be. They also largely endure across time. Comparison, although never straightforward, is not a fanciful endeavour. It allows for certain kings and queens to be regarded afresh and placed in 'underrated' and 'overrated' compartments.

William I (1066–87)

OVERRATED

The English have a strange relationship with their history. No more extreme example of this is where they choose to start it. Most accounts begin with the Battle of Hastings and the Norman Conquest. History kicks off in 1066; everything before that is somewhat murky and only real enthusiasts even attempt to remember the names of monarchs before that point, except for Alfred the Great (who allegedly burnt the cakes) and possibly Cnut (who supposedly issued instructions to the tide, but this was an attempt to demonstrate the limitations of his authority). Edward the Confessor may receive an honourable mention, but only in the context of preparing the ground for the arrival of William I.

If you take a step back, this is a very odd way of looking at things indeed. What happened in 1066 was a massive defeat. Harold Godwinson (who took an arrow in the eye, it is suggested, but that is not certain) was very much the (relatively speaking) English contender to the throne. The aftermath of his death and the triumph of the Normans was utterly catastrophic not only to the English nobility but to Englishness all round.

The country was a victim of a form of ethnic cleansing and to an extent rarely seen anywhere else in Europe for a very long period before or since. Yet our history skirts over that. William somehow becomes an honorary Englishman from the moment that he takes the Crown, the Norman takeover of England is portrayed as a castle-building exercise, the Bayeaux Tapestry is regarded as gospel truth and not a piece of propaganda, and Domesday Book, probably the most recalled element of William's tenure, is treated as an advanced form of accounting to be applauded.

There is, to put mildly, another way of looking at matters. It is that if English history is to be awarded a starting date at all, it should not be in 1066 but either much earlier or after the alien Normans left. William I (the Conqueror) should not be seen in any positive light at all but as a very bad experience.

William's heritage sheds light on an era in which violence was the norm in politics. What came to be called the 'Normans' were a set of Vikings who marched on Paris in 911 and would not leave until the King of France, then Charles III or Charles 'the Simple', handed over territory to them. He held a meeting with the leader of this band of outlaws and eventually decided to offer them land which the chroniclers described as 'Normandie', if their chief (who was dubbed 'Rollo' in Latin, but that was not his name) agreed to be the king's notional vassal and to convert to Christianity. That exchange done, the 'Normans' became part of the extremely complicated French patchwork quilt.

William himself was born more than a century after that bargain. His father, Robert, was the Duke of Normandy but had achieved that status by murdering his uncle and possibly an older brother too. His mother, Herleva, was the daughter of a strikingly wealthy family. They were an admirable match but with one issue of some importance. They were not married. William was therefore illegitimate, and this was not a particular secret. His father wanted to depart for what would inevitably be a long pilgrimage to Jerusalem in 1034 and needed his domestic affairs in order in advance of leaving. He persuaded, probably by sheer force, the nobility of Normandy to accept William as his heir (although this was hardly par for the course, allowing for the fact that he was clearly born out of wedlock) and headed east, only to die on his travels a year later. William, aged about 7, became Duke of Normandy.

This was an extremely exposed title to hold. There were outside interests circling his terrain (the King of France and others with substantial land who liked the notion of additional gains) as well as many within Normandy itself who saw him as an improper figure. He had a series of guardians who sought, with varying degrees of effort, to look after his interests and at least three of them died as they strived to do so. It was a small miracle that William made it to adulthood. Even when he did, his legitimacy (personal and political) remained dubious. In 1049, he sought out a marriage, to Matilda, who had a sizeable stake in Flanders which was of serious value, but the Pope forbade it. William waited a little while and then proceeded with the wedding anyway, irrespective of the Pope's position. It turned out to be a productive pairing as she bore him at least nine children (four of them sons), which as we believe that she was only 4ft 2in tall must have been difficult.

There are three factors to William's rise which are worthy of attention and set the scene for how he should be looked at as a monarch. They are what happened in 1066, his approach to his new realm after becoming king and, briefly, how one should think of Domesday Book if that is his legacy.

William did not become an especially important actor outside of Normandy (where he struggled to impose himself anyway) until after 1060. That date marks the moment at which two major rivals (the King of France and the Count of Anjou) die and their successors have not yet established themselves. William invades the county of Matine and positions himself for obtaining England. The king there, Edward the Confessor, looks very likely to die childless. He was William's cousin, once removed, as William's grandmother had been Edward's mother (she was an astonishing woman, daughter of the Norman ruler Richard the Fearless, married to not one but two English monarchs, and Queen Consort of Denmark and Norway too). Edward had, it was asserted, nominated William as his successor. This was a stretch in terms of the bloodline, but Edward's court had a strong Norman influence over it (courtesy of his mother). The alternative option (arguably with a weaker blood claim but a domestic man of standing) was Harold Godwinson, Edward's brother-in-law. He had, it was contended, sworn to support William as king, although this pledge, if made, occurred after he had been a virtual prisoner of the Duke of Normandy and so was not in the best place to assert his outlook. On his deathbed, Edward, it is said, switched his backing to Harold.

At a minimum this was not a clear-cut situation. There were others who could see themselves as the king as well. They included the de facto king of what we would now call Norway and another with a similar standing in Denmark. For the previous 100 years or more, the English had been open to attack from various subsections of the Vikings and more recently the likes of the Normans. There was no way in which the death of Edward the Confessor would simply usher in a peaceful change.

The duke was prepared, and it turned out that he was fortunate. He had a fleet ready to sail from Normandy in August 1066. If he had been able to leave when he wished, that might have been fatal. Harold, who had been crowned king, was aware of his intentions and even where he might disembark once he reached the south coast of England, and he was ready for him (the quality of intelligence and communications in what seems such a primitive age was actually staggering). If battle had taken place that summer, then not only might Harold have won, but William might also have died.

William I (1066–87)

The weather had other ideas. This was not the best of summers to traverse the Channel. William had to wait for weeks on end for a favourable climate. In the meantime, word reached Harold that his other enemy, Harald Hardrada, King of Norway, had assembled a force and was in Yorkshire. Harold marched his men north, travelling at more than 25 miles a day on foot, encountered Harold at the Battle of Stamford Bridge and won a complete victory, killing the King of Norway as part of it. He then had to turn his troops around and head back south, with a slight detour to London.

William was thus able to land unopposed. He was not completely sure what to do next. Did he move inland towards either Winchester or London (the former being more the political capital, the latter the financial one and bigger city) and stretch his supply lines, or did he stay where he was and dig in?

Harold settled the matter for him by getting to Hastings at speed. The fight duly takes place. The (probably exhausted) native soldiers meet their match. Not only does Harold die but so do two of his brothers, so the rival line for the throne is more or less extinguished. However, the win does not wholly settle matters; it took William two more months to make it to London and be accepted and crowned king. Even then, there were many prominent personalities outside of the capital who did not bend to him.

That is why the second part of William's record is so important. This really was a conquest. It was much more than that in many respects. Between 1066 and 1071 there were several revolts against someone who was seen as a foreign interloper. The one best cited in history is that of Hereward the Wake, but he was far from alone. William moved back and forth between Normandy and England depending on the urgency of the uprisings but otherwise relied on his brother-in-law, Odo of Bayeux, newly minted Earl of Kent, to oversee military matters. Rebellion was never totally wiped out, but it was contained.

This could only be managed by brute force. Foreign nobles and mercenaries had to be co-opted and they would all want something tangible for their trials and tribulations. What they got was England. The former ruling class was pushed to one side. Its lands were distributed to the agents of what was a new master. By the end of his reign, all but two of William's tenants-in-chief were French in origin. A similar strategy was adopted for the Church, with the Pope accepting a massive purge of the bishops so that by the time that William died, the English element of the clergy had all but disappeared. This was critical because the men of the cloth were intermediaries between the ruler and the ruled. Their shift in composition was socially significant. The English peasantry found themselves with an entirely novel (and less benign) set of superiors. What is more, the invaders spoke French to one another and wrote in Latin. Traditional English was a second-class language. These were two very different worlds.

The intensity of this change tends to be underplayed in conventional English history. It was rape and pillage (often literally but also metaphorically). A culture was being decimated. The construction of castles was not motivated by architectural innovation but to set up a base from which the country around it, and the people who lived there, could be terrorised into submission. William was not only a conqueror, he and his men ravaged and savaged what it meant to be English, draining hundreds of years of Anglo-Danish inheritance away. This was an occupation of a semi-totalitarian character.

Yet that is somehow set to one side and William is placed in memory as if the first 'English' king. One distinguished historian, Richard Southern, described what was witnessed in the two decades after Harold was slain at Hastings as 'the single most radical change in European history between the fall of

Rome and the twentieth century'.[2] If he is even half right, then William I was not merely a conqueror, he was Pol Pot with a palace. This was 'Year Zero' for Englishness. It would be more than three centuries before there was a king (Henry IV) born in England with English as his first tongue. One can debate whether this means William I was 'overrated', but he was no friend to England.

The last part for which he is hailed in folk memory is for Domesday Book. This was remarkable. It was an inventory of more than 45,000 land holdings in 14,000 locations. There had been nothing like it before in England (or, as far as it is possible to understand, Europe) before and it would be centuries before anything like it was produced again. It was also compiled in less than a year. It would form two enormous books which were kept at the royal treasury at Winchester and occasionally put on show.

The reason why the information could be collated at such a pace and with such detail is that those whom William had put in charge of England (almost every single man French) had such raw control over their jurisdictions. The data was sitting there waiting for someone to demand it. The purpose of Domesday Book was not to be a historical document or an economics textbook but to set out, at the behest of William I, who had what, what the value of land and other possessions had been thought to be before 1066 and what it was worth in 1086. By such means, the king and his successors, as William died only a year later, would know where they stood in terms of possible taxes.

Having placed William the Conqueror in the right context, how does he measure up as a monarch?

---

[2] *Oxford Essential Quotations* (6th edition), edited by Susan Ratcliffe (2018).

Professional Standing

The professional standing of William I would have depended almost entirely on whether one had been part of the historic English ruling elite before late 1066 or one of the new ruling class, who would come after the Conqueror had seized England and turned the nation upside down.

What is clear is that William's rule never went uncontested. There were several revolts in the first five years of his tenure, a brief interlude of calm, and then a dangerous rebellion in 1075 (the Revolt of the Earls). Matters were not stable even a decade later when William had been the monarch for almost twenty years, as he had to gather a collection of mercenaries in 1085 to quash discontent (paying for these men was one of the motives behind the commissioning of Domesday Book). At least a section of the English never accepted that the Normans were entitled to control the country.

Running both Normandy and England was not a comfortable exercise. William crossed the Channel on twenty or more occasions in his attempt, as he might have seen it, to impose order on one or the other of his territories. There is no doubt as to what was his highest priority. It was Normandy, which was open to interference and more from either the King of France or the Count of Anjou (sometimes both of them with other more minor actors seeking to secure assets as well). For most of the stretch from 1071 to 1084, William was primarily in Normandy, not England, and he was there to defend it.

This meant that he was an absentee figure except when the English were engaged in insurrection to a degree that required his personal intervention. For most of this time, the man in charge on a day-to-day basis was Odo of Bayeux, William's brother-in-law, sometimes assisted by William FitzOsbern. This arrangement was not always a happy one. William would have Odo arrested in 1082. Yet in practical terms it seems to have been effective, if not appealing if one were English in origins. Odo oversaw the total obliteration of English influence in the aristocracy, solicited the aid of the Pope in a complete transformation of the Church and drove the English language out of official favour.

This marginalisation of England was paradoxical. It was a much more impressive asset in terms of its size and status than Normandy, a neutral, rational assessment might have concluded, but it was not treated that way by William or those around him. Normandy was by far the more important. England existed to assist William in his command over Normandy and, as his reign went on, as part of his competition with the French king. William kept the administration of his domains distinct from one another. There was little thought about whether it might be smarter to combine them in some way. In terms of structure, the governance of England under the Anglo-Saxons had been relatively solid by continental standards, so William largely kept it intact, but he introduced Normans everywhere. How well they understood what they had under their authority is suspect. They probably did not care. These were the spoils of war, reinforced by repression; what had come before was of no relevance.

Public Opinion

The state of opinion polling in late eleventh-century England was not well developed. What ordinary people probably thought is unavoidably a matter of speculation. It is not that hard, though, to guess.

The regime change which was pressed on England after 1066 is highly unlikely to have been loved. Life for the peasantry would not have been enchanting beforehand, but the new age would have been worse. For the bottom tier, it would have had no blessings to it at all (Domesday Book reveals that 10 per cent of the population were not just serfs but outright slaves). Whenever a local noble (or more probably a noble who had been displaced or was soon to be removed) rose up against the Normans, they do not seem to have had many difficulties rallying troops to their standard. They all failed, in large part because the Normans had totally rewritten the rulebook through their castles. Public opinion could be whatever it was. The Normans would be hard to throw out by the English alone. Their best hope was in an external invasion, with the King of Denmark (Sweyn II) a possibility. He would have been a foreigner too, but the Scandinavians were less 'foreign' than men of Normandy. If public opinion had counted for anything, William the Conqueror would have had a short tenure.

Financial Competence

England's primary value to William was as a war chest. It had a respectably organised means of mass taxation. Its monarchs, unless inept or inclined to spend too much money on unrewarding fights, were usually well off by the conventions of the day. The Danegeld (essentially protection money presented as a tax to avoid raids on land and property by the Vikings) was well entrenched, so William retained it. Dispossessed nobles or senior men within the Church were a source of reward, so a cut was taken off their former terrain before it was handed on to (Norman) others. The royal estates and forest lands could also be turned into money-spinners. Funds became harder to tap towards what would be the final years of William's reign (mainly because they had been exploited to the full earlier when Normandy was under threat), which made the creation of Domesday Book a worthwhile innovation. Overall, it would be unfair not to describe the new king and those who acted for him as financially competent, but it was a competence whose output was to bleed England dry. Once the full implications of Domesday Book had been digested, more taxation would be sought. The new ruling class would not want for luxury. The overthrown English nobility were worse off for it.

Foreign Policy

The politics of this period was predominantly about France, and it had some confusing features to it. The King of France was rather more than a first among equals, even when his own terrain and wealth were less in scale than those of the rulers of Aquitaine, Anjou and even Normandy, who were, strictly speaking, underlings who were obliged to pay tribute to him and salute him as their senior. William's foreign policy consisted mostly of attempting to keep King Philip I of France at a distance. William met his death while in conflict with the French king's armies (not aided, as the next section will illuminate, by his own eldest son being more than willing to conspire with the French monarch when that suited).

William was, nonetheless, a canny player in these matters. He used his large number of children as tools in dynastic activities conducted through marriage, and that applied to his grandchildren as well (it was perfectly common then for marriages to be agreed when those to be wed were very little). He did his best to ally with the Holy Roman Emperor as part of his containment of France. He was closely linked to Flanders through his own relatives, and Flanders was becoming a vital political actor. He courted the Pope, whose backing was essential if his drive to take over the English Church was to be as absolute as he wanted it to be. Yet try as he might, Normandy was hard to defend adequately. At no point could William, even with England as his backstop, be totally confident of his hold over it. This made England all the more useful, as it was, realistically, beyond the reach of the French king.

Succession

With four sons and five daughters (perhaps more), William might have deemed succession one of his less pressing problems. The truth was the opposite. Exactly how land was distributed after the death of a king was never a matter of consensus, and diplomacy was not the only method of deciding who would be left with what, especially as England as well as Normandy would be available for inheriting.

William had an extremely uneasy relationship with his eldest son, Robert. He suspected his motives and would not allow him access to either a sizeable amount of money, or titles, or any authority. The two men literally came to blows, such was the scale of their mutual animosity. Robert had colluded with the French king and made a bond with Odo of Bayeux, the individual with the most power in England when William was not there (which was much of the time), which made the king concerned about him as well. Nor was Robert close to either of his most important brothers, William and Henry.

So, the succession which William would settle on was imperfect and unstable. Robert was to be made the Duke of Normandy, the most prestigious of the old king's domains, but would not be king in England. That honour was to fall to the next son in line (William II or William Rufus) with the faint assumption that were he to die childless then the next oldest brother, Henry, would come after him.

This was not a bargain which Robert would be content with. He wanted the lot. Between 1087 and 1096, the Duke of Normandy looked for whatever openings he could find to undermine William II. He never accepted William's right to rule in England. He would in later life be joined in this scheming by his own son, also William. This was a family feud with serious ramifications for England as a country.

William I (1066–87)

It would eventually reach a conclusion but not through negotiation. After William II's mysterious death in the New Forest (for which there was no shortage of conspiracy theories at the time), Henry moved first and fastest to stake his claim for a coronation. Robert did not appreciate his footwork. He would head to England in an attempt to reverse the succession by arms. He harried Henry regularly for the initial several years of his tenure. Henry avoided taking part in the First Crusade because to be out of England then would have been to give a hostage to fortune (Robert, by contrast, did sign up for it).

The battle of the brothers only ended with Henry carrying the day at the Battle of Tinchebrai in 1106. Robert was not just defeated, he was captured. He would be kept as a prisoner in Cardiff Castle for almost thirty years afterwards. His son, William, sought to take up his cause, but Henry saw him off.

This was a brutal final stage to what is a cruel episode in English history. William I should be seen in the light of what was a terrible episode for the English people, be they rich or poor. His standing is overrated because the nature of his time as king and what happened on his orders are diminished. His birth meant he was known as 'William the Bastard'. The English had reason to call him that as well.

Stephen (1135–54)

UNDERRATED

Historians of the Middle Ages have taken an intense interest in Stephen and his reign. The wider public has not. For someone who was on the throne for almost twenty years, he attracts surprisingly little focus. If he is recalled at all, it is as a man who pushed himself forward to be king when there was another figure, Matilda, daughter of Henry I, who in blood terms had a stronger claim on the throne than Stephen did but was denied it, or so the standard interpretation runs, because of her gender. This has rendered Stephen as at best ungallant and at worst the deliberate beneficiary of discrimination. No other person who has been anywhere close to the Crown since his death in 1154 has come by the name Stephen. It is as if he had tainted it so thoroughly as to make it out of bounds to royals forever.

This, however, is rather harsh. As will be set out here, there was far more to the dispute over the succession than simple sexism (although it would be naïve to deny that this played a part in the saga). Stephen was frequently extraordinarily benign towards those who took up against him (while demonstrating indifference towards some of those who followed him, needlessly turning friends into enemies). The deal that he would eventually do with the future Henry II has no equivalent in English history. It is he who is the last Norman monarch and the one there to usher in the 331-year rule of the Plantagenets. He is a fascinating character and as a monarch had more to commend him than he is credited with.

Stephen was the younger son of Stephen, Count of Blois, who was married to Adele, a daughter of William the Conqueror. She must have been a formidable force because when her husband arrived home early from the First Crusade, having found a military campaign of this type not to his liking, she could not bear the implicit cowardice this was seen to involve and sent him back to the front again. He promptly died in 1102 as fighting clearly was not his forte. That left Stephen as a junior son. His eldest brother, William, seems to have had some kind of mental incapacity and he drops out of history. Another male sibling, Odo, would die comparatively young (as a teenager), but there was an older brother still, Theobald of Blois, who, in blood terms and ranking for the English Crown, was higher.

Stephen, then aged around 6, was taken in by Henry I, now English king, and treated as if one of his own. The patronage awarded to him was considerable. He soon became extremely wealthy but was not thought of as destined to be a contender for the throne as there were others ahead of him in that context (not least his own brother, if the throne were to head down that line at some moment). He would become even better placed in terms of his affluence and influence due to a marriage that was encouraged by Henry to Matilda of Boulogne in 1125. She came with estates in Boulogne itself but also in Kent, adjacent to where Stephen had been the recipient of lands courtesy of the king. This meant that he was a pivotal player in cross-Channel commercial trade and so became further enriched.

He was not the only member of his family to have reason to be grateful to Henry. Another of Stephen's brothers, and at times his close collaborator, Henry of Blois, also had the monarch's kindly attention. He would be placed in the Church and promoted rapidly through the ranks to be the Abbot of Glastonbury and Bishop of Winchester; these titles were not only prized but came with a huge sum of land and money as well. Henry may have been the richest man in the kingdom after the monarch (and perhaps also Stephen). Why Theobald did not do as well is uncertain, but it could have been because it was believed that as the eldest remaining son, he would inherit some large terrain from his mother's side of the family.

There was another, fundamentally important individual at court, until his untimely death removed him. Prince William was the only son of Henry I and acknowledged almost universally as his heir. He would drown when the *White Ship* sank in 1120, leaving a single survivor. This threw the regime into chaos. It could have been even more devastating to the lineage because Stephen had been scheduled to be on the same ship as well, but he missed the boat and so did not perish. Henry had no male heir, only a daughter, Matilda. He remarried but did not produce any further children. He spent his last few years seeking to make Matilda secure in her right to come after him. This would never be uncontested.

To comprehend Stephen as king therefore requires three elements to be inspected. The first is what happened in 1135. The second is how he handled himself during the civil war. The last is his own exit.

Henry I died suddenly and unexpectedly in 1135. Matilda and her husband, Geoffrey, were in Anjou. Stephen moved at high speed, heading to London in a bid to be crowned. He had strong support in that city and enough nobles behind him to take the throne. If his brother Theobald had been equally quick, then there would have been a real struggle over who became the king, as Theobald was a contender with some potentially important allies. Possession turned out to be nine-tenths of the law in 1135.

Stephen acted as he did despite all that he had owed the late king for his rise and his public pledge of recognition for Matilda as Henry's heir, which had been made some eight years earlier. His shift of opinion did not do much for his reputation in some quarters. His foes argued that he was an untrustworthy usurper. An effort was made to assert that Henry had changed his mind at the last minute in favour of Stephen over Matilda, but there were no plausible witnesses to this improbable final decision.

In truth, the rules of the succession in these conditions and where the dead king had possessions in both England and France were ambiguous. Matilda's sex was obviously a matter for consideration. Here, too, precedent was very patchy. There were parts of France and elsewhere in Europe where a woman could inherit titles and land, and rule in her own right if no male heir were on hand. There were other locations where titles could change hands, but the husband would be expected to take charge. And there were instances, most prominently involving the French throne itself, where Salic Law was applied and it would not be possible for a woman to be the outright Queen of France, only a queen consort (this did not prevent the English later insisting that Mary II, Anne and even Victoria were the proper 'Kings of France', even though it was nonsense on the facts). Opinions would have varied as to which formula should be applied to Matilda. There should have been rather less discussion as to whether Stephen was younger or older than his brother Theobald, but his sibling seems to have accepted his exclusion and sought instead to take over Normandy.

Matilda's power was weakened by what turned out to be a politically maladroit second marriage. She had been wed first to Henry V, the Holy Roman Emperor. When he died in 1125, she was a valuable woman to marry, and Geoffrey of Anjou was her suitor. This was not the most inspired of alliances. Anjou and Normandy had long clashed with one another, and the two clans thought of themselves as enemies. If Matilda became queen,

Stephen (1135–54)

then it was assumed that Geoffrey would be the real monarch. This was forcefully opposed by a major segment of the Norman Establishment, which explains why they embraced Stephen despite his shaky claim to England. If Matilda had married a less contentious man, then she might, admittedly only might, have become the full-blown queen her father wanted.

The earliest years of Stephen's tenure passed off relatively peacefully. His grasp on power was not a subject of substantial challenge. He kept potentially difficult barons quiet, soothed the top ranks of the clergy (with the assistance of his brother Henry) and made peace with Louis VI of France, who had the capacity to make life challenging for him. The Scottish border, a back door to the English throne, was stable for a while. Geoffrey and Matilda were marooned in France and had no invasion strategy.

All of this was to change radically. This was partly because Stephen himself made serious errors. When the then Archbishop of Canterbury died not long after he had become king, Stephen snatched his lands and aggrieved his brother Henry by not promoting him to the most elevated post in the Church, as the latter plainly thought would happen. The preconditions for a rebellion were coming good.

When the clash came, it was on several fronts. Matilda formally declared herself the rightful queen. Her husband invaded Normandy. Robert of Gloucester, her half-brother, charged in from the west. David I, King of Scotland and Matilda's uncle, came across the border with a threatening army. He was initially repelled at the Battle of the Standard in 1138, but he was strong enough, along with own son, Henry, to settle himself in at Carlisle and oblige Stephen to bargain with him. Stephen's brother Henry was still fuming about having been denied the see of Canterbury and could not be counted on.

It very nearly all came crashing down for Stephen. He was fighting on too many fronts. He tried to shore himself up by handing out new titles to nobles who might be inclined to stick with him, but as an approach that had its limitations. There were two rival courts in England (Stephen's the bigger).

He was defeated and captured at the Battle of Lincoln in 1141 and locked up inside Bristol Castle. Matilda appeared to have the path to the throne in front of her. She made too hasty decisions that alienated some crucial nobles from her. Henry, still Bishop of Winchester, appointed himself as the go-between to seek some sort of accord between her and Stephen, but his efforts got him nowhere. The citizenry of London was notably determined not to allow Matilda to enter the city and be crowned.

A strong set of cards was played very poorly. Matilda lost the initiative. Robert of Gloucester was then himself taken prisoner after the Rout of Winchester by William of Ypres, an ally of Stephen. The two men were traded, and Stephen was in the driving seat. He had himself crowned as king again. He had the chance to seize Matilda on a number of occasions but preferred to allow her free passage out of England. Geoffrey of Anjou calculated that he was better off raiding France instead (he would take Normandy in 1144). The Scots were bought off by being granted a section of northern England (although this annoyed others who felt that they should have that land). Stephen and his brother Henry patched matters up. The arrival of the Second Crusade would distract some nobles from the affairs of England as they headed for the Holy Land in search of divine approval. Stephen had won.

Except that it was his turn to blow it. Stephen fell out with some substantial members of the nobility. He acquired the disconcerting habit of summoning people who thought he was their friend and ally to his court and then arresting them. He made it clear that he expected his son Eustace to succeed after him, but he was a widely disliked individual because of heavy taxes he imposed in his own lands. The chances of Matilda overthrowing him were nevertheless still small. Her young eldest son, Henry, was more viable. He was not the damaged goods that his father was, nor was his gender a complication. After his marriage to

Stephen (1135–54)

Eleanor of Aquitaine, he was a seriously appealing prospect. The civil war would be revived again.

The final twist in the succession, which reflects well on Stephen, will be set out later. It was preceded by generosity towards those sworn against him that was astonishing. In 1147, the youthful Prince Henry arrived in England at the head of a small and not especially intimidating band of mercenaries. It was not long before he had run out of money to pay them and had not found enough bounty on his travels as another form of compensation. Stephen stepped in by settling his debts and allowing Henry to return to France safely. Another incursion in 1149 ended without Stephen inflicting the kind of punishment on Henry and his followers which he could have done. This pattern would repeat itself in what would become the succession endgame in 1153–54. Stephen's charitable behaviour might have been a reflection of his overall good nature but was probably due to his being aware of how well Henry I had treated him, and being reluctant to see his daughter or grandson come to any harm.

This was a prelude to one of the most exceptional transfers of power in English history (although it required the death of one of the primary players to oil the opportunity). Just in terms of this event, Stephen may be deemed an underrated monarch. He was not one of the best but does not do badly on the metrics.

Professional Standing

As is implicit in the previous narrative, Stephen's standing varied considerably. At the top of his game, he was a mighty figure in the land. At his most petty, he was his own worst enemy and a liability.

He started well and had a revival in the early 1140s, but civil war would be corrosive to his position. Unless he could resolve his right to be king and either defeat alternative claimants or send them away packing, then the chances of decent public appointments in England were slim. His command over the Church would have been more compelling if had not slighted his own brother and then a decade or so later fallen into a disagreement with the Pope that again should have been averted.

At his best, he was a very sound monarch. He mostly retained Henry I's policy of making meritocratic appointments. He was well served by his younger brother (when they did not disagree about who should be the Archbishop of Canterbury) and was also enlightened in other choices such as placing Waleran of Beaumont in high office. He bought himself some political space by establishing new titles which would then be distributed to nobles in exchange for their fidelity. This was not without some cost as well as benefits, but it led him recover from the events of 1141.

Repeated bouts of civil conflict still stack up against him. While England was not in as bad a condition as later Victorian scholars of the time would contend (they referred to it as 'the Anarchy'), there are contemporary accounts which suggest that it was recognised that the realm was not in a good place (although who should be blamed for this depended on whether one was allied to him or Matilda). Towards the end of his reign, Stephen seemed to become a shrewder operator. An attempt was led to repair the broken structure of government. The restive Scots seemed to be appeased. In a clever dynastic gambit, his son Eustace was married to Constance, the sister of Louis VII, which won him over. All of this would eventually come to naught, once a rejuvenated Henry, son of Matilda, was on the horizon.

Public Opinion

Documentation which would provide data on the public perceptions of Stephen is hard to obtain. The best that can be deduced is that he was popular at the beginning of his reign and at its end but that the hard middle years which saw civil war would not make for a satisfied mass population.

Stephen seems to have been consistently more popular in London than anywhere of note elsewhere. Along with Robert of Gloucester becoming an option for a hostage swap, it was probably his popularity in London that saved the king when Matilda had England in the palm of her hand, only then to make too many enemies. Stephen certainly cultivated the merchants and the emerging networks within London with vigour. It was he who preferred to operate from Westminster rather than Winchester, and this would prove to be part of his legacy. In his final eighteen months or so as king, he threw himself earnestly into finding a solution to the civil war that would endure, and so at his death he was probably a popular man again. He was, apparently, an easy-going individual, modest in his private dealings and pious in his religion.

Financial Competence

Stephen started off in an immensely favourable place financially. He had become extremely rich due to the attention paid to him by Henry I and a smart marriage. Henry I died with the Treasury in an encouraging order. There was plenty of money in the bank at the time that Stephen became king.

It would not be there for very long. In order to placate nobles who were not completely convinced that he should be on the throne, and the marauding Scottish king and prince in the north, Stephen had to empty his coffers. He would also need mercenaries from overseas (there were many of them assisting various contestants for England at this time) and they were an expensive acquisition. Once Stephen started spending, he seems to have found it hard to impose financial discipline later. None of this was helped once the civil war began to take its toll and the solicitation of revenue suffered. Barely five years after he was crowned, Stephen was a bankrupt in all but name. A by-product of this was that the royal monopoly over the coinage, which was a crucial aspect of monarchy, had been interrupted. Many a noble had simply created their own coins which, in their home area, would be as attractive as Stephen's.

Like everything else to do with his reign, Stephen's financial rectitude relied on an easing of civil disputes and an end to an atmosphere of lawlessness that went beyond the issue of who the monarch should be. As with other areas, an order of sorts awaited an overarching political outcome. When that materialised, Stephen sought to take back the coinage as his own and with some success. If he had lived until 1164 rather than 1154, he might have made a meaningful difference to the situation. As it was, he had made enough progress and limited his expenditures to such an extent that Henry II would not become the king an impoverished figure. Even in a short passage of time, there had been enough of a restoration of the currency and sufficient administrative reforms to have an effect on the state of England. Stephen was not as clever a steward of national wealth as Henry I proved to be, but he was not feckless.

Foreign Policy

Stephen had too much on his plate to allow him to devise diplomatic innovations on any scale or to interfere in the domestic politics of other places. To that extent, one might state that he did not have a foreign policy. This would be too sweeping, but of necessity he had to take care in his calculations.

In ordinary conditions, France and its various contingent parts would have been at the heart of any foreign policy in the twelfth century. Stephen was in no position to act decisively over the Channel. He could not defend Normandy or make progress in Anjou or Aquitaine without troops on the ground and he did not have them. All he could do was seek to keep his losses to an acceptable minimum, which was not straightforward. He did his best to appease the King of France and avoided his wrath. Had Paris come out robustly for Matilda, that would have been a feather in her cap of political value.

In these less than ideal decades, avoiding foreign policy engagements was perhaps the best approach. Henry did not involve himself with the Holy Roman Emperor, as his predecessor had done. He was not enamoured of the thought of putting on armour and heading towards Jerusalem when others involved in the civil war at home or on the continent found the Second Crusade (1147–50) an honourable cause. Such an excursion would have been madness when Stephen was not in full control of England. Chivalry could wait while the Scots and other menaces were bought off. It might not have been dignified, but it was a pragmatic plan for a foreign policy.

Succession

At the beginning of 1153, the succession in England still resembled a stalemate. Some of the most significant figures had left the scene. Robert of Gloucester, an important agent of Matilda, was dead. Geoffrey of Anjou had expired in 1151. Count Theobald of Blois, the eldest brother of Stephen whom he had brushed aside in 1135, had died in 1152 (although he had sons who might have made an advance on the throne if they could have found a constituency to cheer them on). Matilda remained alive (she did not pass away until 1167), but she had run out of steam as a potential queen in her own name and was now prepared to permit her son Henry, the rising star of the age, to be the pretender instead.

It did not look as if he would secure the throne without a massive intervention of fate. Stephen was devoted to the idea that

Eustace would be the next king and sought to sign up nobles to his cause. There was a further son, William, who would need to be a beneficiary in terms of land after the loss of his father. To marginalise them, the aspiring Henry II would probably have to succeed in combat.

That is what looked as if it would happen. Henry, whose previous missions to England had been a fiasco, chanced his arm again in 1153. Once more, planning and execution were distant cousins. His ship was taken off course by the wind and he found himself disembarking with his men in Dorset.

A showdown was expected. Henry took his troops to Malmesbury, yet a battle there was impractical. He then appeared at Wallingford, where it appeared that a fight to the death to be king beckoned.

It did not. Eustace, the chosen heir, had died and his distraught father had to reconsider the succession. The understandable response would have been to recruit Prince William as his heir on bloodline. The desirable outcome for England as a whole, nonetheless, would bring Henry into the fold.

That is exactly what Stephen did. Instead of taking up arms at Wallingford, Stephen invited Henry to a one-on-one deliberation. They agreed on what would become the Treaty of Winchester. The old king would remain on the throne for the remainder of his natural days. His son William would then inherit his personal land but not the throne. Henry would take the Crown in a smooth succession.

That an agreement of this character could be reached at all was not to be anticipated (although it was close as a blueprint to one that Henry, Bishop of Winchester, had placed before Matilda in 1141). That it would be done so graciously was staggering. Stephen paraded Henry through Winchester as if he were his own son and repeated the trick in London. William was brought into the arrangement but as Earl of Surrey, not King of England, and he collaborated with Henry II without rancour until he died five years into his reign (to be replaced as Count of Boulogne, ironically, by a woman, his sister Marie).

Whether this peace would have endured had Stephen not died in 1154 is worthy of speculation. It is possible that the king might have thought again or that William would not have tolerated his place in the new constitutional order. It did, though, finish a debilitating conflict on coherent terms. Henry II would be the first Plantagenet king. Stephen has been underrated for allowing this to happen.

Henry II (1154–89)

UNDERRATED

Henry II may be (perhaps dimly) remembered as the first Plantagenet monarch. The episode with which he is most closely associated is the murder of Thomas Becket in 1170, an event which he felt obliged to offer penance for in its immediate aftermath and for which he has been paying fines in terms of his popular reputation ever since. Critics of his reign might also place weight on the fact that his estranged wife and at least three of his sons rose up against him several times and were willing to align with the notional King of France (Louis VII, who did not control anything like the borders of modern France) and, on occasion, although not with much advantage to him, the King of Scotland. The breadth of that coalition might suggest that Henry II was not much of a king. This is a falsehood.

It was not absolutely inevitable that he would become king at all. He was the eldest son of the second marriage of Matilda, daughter of Henry I, who, as the previous chapter has outlined, tried to become ruler of England in her own right but failed in large part due to her gender. Her marriage to Geoffrey of Anjou must also have counted against her as he was not the most diplomatic of men and Anjou was a powerful force in itself, which nobles in England would have been extremely wary of.

Henry was committed to supporting his mother and her claim. He was also precocious about it. He made his first foray into England and its peculiar politics in 1141–42 before the age of 10 but did not spend long there once he had exhibited his credentials. He would, exceptionally optimistically, arrive again, barely a teenager, in 1147 at the head of a small band of mercenaries, but he clearly had no flair for petty cash as he ran out of the resources required to satisfy his troops strikingly swiftly. He had to be bailed out by King Stephen and allowed to head back to the Channel with a safe passage. This was, to put it mildly, honourable of a sovereign whom Henry was aspiring to unseat. A different king would at the least have captured him and insisted on a ransom for his liberty or been within his rights, under the laws of war as they stood then, to have him killed. History would have changed.

In the mistaken hope of third time lucky in winning hearts and minds (or just a single battle of note), Henry would throw the dice in England once more, this time in alliance with the King of Scotland. This did not work out for the best either. He could have met his death again without good fortune.

So, Henry, the would-be King of England, had to build up his power base in France if he were to be a credible champion of his mother and become a contender for the throne himself (although his two sly younger brothers might not let that pass unchallenged). He was appointed Lord of Normandy in 1150 at the behest of his father and then, when that parent expired in 1151, he succeeded him as the Count of Anjou. At least in terms of its treasury (although this triggered envy and suspicion in England), this was a serious springboard for the succession. He could afford mercenaries now.

His absolutely brilliant move across the dynastic chess board came a year later. Louis VII had been married to Eleanor of

Aquitaine. She had come with an astonishing dowry (including the lands of Aquitaine itself). By their union, Louis VII had vastly improved his overall position as a landlord.

After fourteen years together, she had not produced a son for him. Louis seems to have concluded that the blame for this lay with her. He manufactured a divorce on overtly spurious arguments. He was compelled to release her with her territories intact, as before their wedding. A mere eight weeks after he had done so, Henry, eleven years her junior, saw off a swarm of suitors (including, it is said, his own younger brother) to take her hand. That the divorce settlement indicated that she could not take a new husband without the assent of her recently departed one was ignored (and whether the terms were that unambiguous is debatable). Henry had Eleanor and through her Aquitaine, and by that liaison, he arguably had more terrain in what is now France than Louis VII. His audacity did not win him friends in Paris. Louis looked like something of a fool, and he regarded the whole saga as an insult. It probably did not assist his mood that despite being in her thirties, Eleanor gave birth to five children in a mere six years, four of whom were sons (the eldest of which, William, would expire in his infancy). By the mid-1150s, Henry would have appeared a much more impressive option as monarch than he did only a decade earlier. As set out before, he took the throne, without much duress, in October 1154.

To appreciate what would happen after that demands an understanding of three factors: first, the international imperatives for the king in terms of preserving and promoting his (Angevin) empire at that time; second, the reasons why he and Thomas Becket feuded, which would culminate in his former protégé being hacked to death in front of his own altar, in his own cathedral, by four knights; and finally, the innate friction which existed over the future distribution of spoils after Henry II's eventual death. These tempted his eldest son, Henry, then Geoffrey, then Richard and finally John (there would be eight children from his marriage to Eleanor of Aquitaine, all told) to conspire against their father, revolt either individually or collectively on multiple occasions, and eventually force him into submission.

The Plantagenets might have been distinct from the Normans and hence are regarded by history as a new ruling line, but they had something very crucial in common with them. They were French and not English.

France, or more precisely the various territories which largely but not entirely match the borders of contemporary France, was the premier prize in western Europe. This was where the action was at. England brought with it a title with some twinkle and a reasonable revenue stream, but it was a second-tier contender for appeal in Europe. If one can imagine it in the context of the US state of Nevada, it was Reno or Carson City but not Las Vegas. The Normans had operated upon that basis. The early Plantagenets would not deviate from those calculations. They might have had a degree of affection for England and the English, but they could barely speak the language, never mind bring themselves to comprehend a culture which would have appeared backward compared to France.

Henry's initial agenda would be overseas, with Brittany the acquisition which would make his name. He spent a full six and a half years of the initial eight years of his tenure outside of England. He would be away for twenty-one of his thirty-four years at the helm. He was highly effective in his territorial aims and would outwit Louis VII on a regular basis. This meant that he had an empire which was enormous by the standards of its time, but with an array of different customs which had to be part of governance. As Henry was solemn about his duties as well as astute at capturing castles in France, this meant the creation of an improvised form of mobile monarchy, which allowed him to oversee matters to an incredible extent – stunning considering the communication methods of the age and the dismal track record of other kings who had attempted to do something similar. England was part of a wider methodology.

As his reign progressed, Henry would spend more years in England but invariably was lured to France. When his conflict with his family raged out of control, it was in France that the showdowns happened.

A partial exception to that rule involved his volcanic relationship with Thomas Becket. He had made him the Archbishop of Canterbury when that position became vacant, leaning on the papacy (which was suffering from schism) to confirm the appointment. His choice was controversial. Becket had been his chancellor and was seen as Henry's instrument. He was worldly, not godly. This was not unusual among the senior bishops (a sizeable percentage of whom were the illegitimate offspring of kings), but even so, the charge that the freshly arrived archbishop would be a cipher of the throne was out there and this seems to have persuaded Becket that he should be courting Church opinion.

It did not take long for the former allies to become mortal enemies. The initial cause of disagreement was about the comparative authority of the courts of law that were in the orbit of the king and ecclesiastical courts which had historically been institutionally separated. A special bone of contention was what to do with clergy who were accused of criminal activity (often financial misappropriation). Henry wanted them dealt with inside his fiefdom. Becket took a stand against this initiative.

Henry did not pursue his policy with rigorous consistency. He would bend when the Pope suggested dexterity. This was a grey area not just in England but in much of Christendom. The demarcation lines between the Church and State were not as crystal clear as either supporters of the king or the archbishop insisted. Having made some progress, Henry, rapidly tiring of Becket, pressed home his advantage by setting out a rulebook through the Constitutions of Clarendon at a convocation of senior clergy in 1164.

Becket first resisted, then recanted, then recused himself from the deliberations being conducted. It seemed as if Henry would go for broke and put him on trial (and in a secular court to make his point). Becket had no intention of being a martyr – although that would later be his fate – and fled abroad.

He came back out of immense annoyance that there had been a coronation ceremony (of which more to come) which was conducted without, as would be the norm, him being at centre of it. This was a major miscalculation. Brinkmanship could no more be contained. It only took one sentence allegedly expressed by Henry II – 'Will no one rid me of this turbulent priest?' – for those in armour who wanted his favour to take it on themselves to charge to Canterbury and slice up the archbishop. Whether they were acting on express orders, telepathy or their own hoof will never be known. It forced Henry to engage in many rounds of public atonement, make monetary recompense in the shape of religious buildings and ease up on the Church politically. His power was barely scratched.

It was, however, contested by his wife and children, not that they were strongly motivated by any outrage at the treatment of Thomas Becket. Henry had a lot of land and there were, at this juncture but not later, four sons who circled it, wondering how it would be split when he died. They were cheered on by Eleanor of Aquitaine, whose utility to Henry had diminished once she had pulled off the epic feat of providing so many heirs (too many to keep satisfied, it would turn out) in a short stretch of years. She was under a form of house arrest, while he looked elsewhere for female company (which produced a substantial brood of illegitimate children from a small battalion of mistresses). In the midst of all this, Louis VII was attempting to retake via factional plotting among the king's sons what he could not win by means of reconquest. William the Lion of Scotland could also sense opportunity knocking.

Henry II (1154–89)

This alliance rose up in the Great Revolt of 1173. Henry saw it off with comparative ease. There would be several other eruptions, but he would not be done for until virtually at his deathbed. Succession would bedevil him and England (and various parts of France) through his final breath.

Henry was indisputably a man of action and acrimony. Has he been underrated as a monarch?

Professional Standing

Henry may not have been physically in England very much, but in mental terms he was a presence. He had firm objectives in mind for his realm. He was to reassert the authority which Henry I had once enjoyed. He wanted a much more efficient form of royal administration, which could function in his absence. He had a deep personal interest in law and order and the structure of justice. He would come to be regarded as the father of English common law (which has been much admired elsewhere). That he should be intrigued by this and expend substantial personal capital in making it happen fitted a man who, although a giant when it came to the battlefield, was also an uncommonly scholarly monarch.

The first task was to put an end to the disrepair which civil insurrection had caused, a mayhem that historians would refer to ominously as 'the Anarchy'. Certain nobles had overstepped the mark. The standing of the throne had been diminished. A number of unauthorised castles had been erected. The Forest Law had been eroded. Private currencies were in circulation. This all had to be reversed.

The difficulties had been hardened by the lack of highly qualified and suitably motivated men to turn the king's will into reality. Henry was an able talent spotter. He knew that he needed worthy agents to keep the show on the road when he was nearer to the Mediterranean than the River Medway. He wanted to traverse beyond the usual suspects when it came to staffing the monarchy. He reached out to 'new men' of various backgrounds and sorts, in the spirit of meritocracy. This was probably not seen as such a benign move by sections of the nobility, but this king would be hard to challenge.

It was the sanctity of the law that Henry considered central to his strategy. Legislation relating to it needed to be revisited. The structure of the law was also a dog's breakfast, far too disparate in its character. It had to be centralised and become more uniform so that the same law meant the same thing across the entirety of England. This would not happen by itself, nor did the barons, or sheriffs, have many incentives to ensure consistency. This would demand leadership from the top. What transpired was a design in which travelling judges roamed the country to improve the quality of justice on offer. It also meant that trial by jury would be expanded, and this offered some buttress against corruption.

Henry could see virtue in bureaucracy by horseback as that was how he conducted his own affairs. This was a sophisticated system, and it was strong enough to deal with upheaval later in his reign. He was perceived at the time to be an enlightened ruler and eight centuries later that perception still appears valid.

Public Opinion

The records are sketchy and perhaps excessive attention is lavished on the scraps that are available. There does not appear to be much doubt that Henry's ascension to the throne was very popular. He was drawing a line under what had been a damaging and dispiriting fifteen years of internal disputes.

His reforms of the law, in so far as they were contemplated by the average serf, should have been embraced as well. It was the poorest who were the most exposed to arbitrary and chaotic justice. Order and certainty in what would have been highly exposed lives would have been seen as a mercy.

What is harder to consider is the extent to which the Becket murder turned opinion against Henry. It was a scandal that caught the imagination. Whether he was responsible was a matter for conjecture. The Church (manifestly) considered an unauthorised execution of one of its own to be a monstrosity. What their flock felt is more for speculation. Henry's display of remorse, and willingness to open up his coffers as part of that process, would have eased the situation. There was no internal uprising. He and the clergy reached a subsequent understanding. He did not cease to be the dominant individual. He also had pet causes including compensation for the shipwrecked which would have made friends.

This respect for him might also be a clue to why the potentially fatal combination of an unhappy wife, feuding sons, a conspiring French king, an active King of Scotland and a few peeved nobles in Ireland, which on paper must have seemed like an intimidating assortment of enemies, had so little traction.

His military insight – which was truly transfixing – was most of his shield and sword, but an underlying popularity that ran through the social spectrum must have been part of his protection as well. He went out of his way to display that he had the popular touch, which as he was not even English (and this was unavoidably plain) was cheek, affectation or real, but it rallied men to his cause. There is certainly no evidence that when news of his death reached England, it prompted celebrations.

Financial Competence

Henry started his reign as a very rich man, possibly the wealthiest in western Europe. This enabled him to oversee a court (on those occasions when this restless soul was in one place for long enough for a conventional court to occur) that was the wonder of his era. It was also in part a form of job creation scheme at several levels of society. His pockets were always deep enough to reach into. Anjou and Aquitaine alone were enticing equivalents of a current account and a savings account.

This did not mean that taxation was abolished. As part of his drive to reassert monarchical authority, he made a special effort to ensure that the nobility offered up the taxation that it was required to. If feeling in need of some extra sums, the Crown would extract 'gifts' and 'concessions' from its tenants-in-chief, although this may have been as much about reminding those who was the top dog as about the condition of the balance sheet. Taxation was not, however, the cause of agitation.

As with the law, Henry wanted to be a modernising monarch in finance. Again, he sought out 'new men' to operate for him. Accountancy methods were updated. Taxes were collected more effectively and hence at a lesser cost. There was widespread reform of the coinage, which underpinned its value. There would not be a king with as laser-like an interest here until Henry VII (who started poorer). By the yardstick which would be the performance of later Plantagenets, he was the Bill Gates of his era.

Foreign Policy

That effectiveness with funding was often the by-product of his successful foreign policy. If Henry II had been a boxer, then, as an adult, he would not have lost a bout until the last round of his last fight. He was the pre-eminent actor of his age, and this added to the security of his tenure as the monarch.

His initial challenge was to keep hold of what he had obtained in short order before he took the Crown in England, namely Normandy, Anjou and Aquitaine. These alone were critical territories. There were other people, Louis VII, and after him the more cunning Philip II of France, who would make trouble for him. There were wayward brothers at the start and malign sons scheming at the finish. His hold was robust. What would make him even more of an authority was when he became, to all intents and purposes, the overlord of Brittany — another pot of gold, if one could put both hands around it. By a series of salami-slicing moves he would outflank those who had also eyed up Brittany. He could then pick off the odd castle and smaller patches of land, and trade them in as he wanted.

Within the British Isles there were also room for increased prestige and property. William the Lion of Scotland had underestimated Henry and began what would become referred to as the 'Auld Alliance' with France against England, opening a second flank to the north as the Great Revolt began.

It did not do anything for him. His attempt to seize a swathe of northern England ended with his army smashed and he himself captured, paraded in the streets to public mirth and eventually being condemned to acquiesce to the Treaty of Falaise of 1174 and admit that Henry would be his master. Wales did not have a single dissident leader, but there were those who wanted to break out of their semi-independent areas and snatch land which was under the supervision of Henry's men. This did not materialise, and by the end of his reign, Henry held more of Wales than he had when he arrived.

The most substantial Henrician effect was in Ireland. He was somewhat jump-started into activity. What began as an authorised but privatised incursion into hostile Irish territory in 1167 suddenly obtained momentum. Henry did not want to owe his status in Ireland to those who might be flying his flag but had their own interests at heart. He assembled a substantial set of ships and men and made off for Ireland at their helm in 1171. The process of conquest was partial (and not in any way pretty), but when it was concluded and he came back to England six months afterwards, the writ of the Plantagenets ran across Dublin and most of the more agreeable lands beyond it. By accident (in terms of timing) as well as inclination, Henry had imposed England on the Irish people. The ramifications of this over several centuries would be immense, but he was hardly to realise this.

Succession

There have been many moments in history when the absence of an heir, or the sight of a child being thrust onto the throne, have been the cause of consternation. Henry's woes were entirely different.

He had a massive empire and for a substantial period of time four healthy sons who wanted a share of it. In the late twelfth century, there was no formula for what to do about this, hence a dilemma. Should the priority be that the whole of this land was passed on to the eldest son to keep it intact? Should it be passed to one person but not always the eldest, depending on whom the king favoured? Should it be divided up between the sons, and if so, how would that tricky territorial distribution be organised?

Henry might have privately wished to maintain his massive bounty as it was, but there was little or no chance of his stubborn sons assenting to one among their ranks having such a reward given to them. The king started by attempting to charm his eldest son, the younger Henry, with a promise that he would have England, then hardening that offer to include a coronation to that effect while Henry was still alive, as a practical demonstration of what he was entitled to. In what was the only occasion of its form in England (there was more of a track record for it in parts of France), Henry junior went through a coronation service not merely once in Westminster in 1170, becoming the notional King of England, Duke of Normandy and Count of Anjou, but also (on what basis remains bewildering) once again in 1172 (in Winchester) in tandem with his marriage to Margaret of France. Still not pleased, he died in 1183. His brother Geoffrey expired in 1186, which cut the sons who needed succour to Richard and John.

That should have made life less painful. It did not. It was suggested to Richard that he could now be crowned pseudo-King of England and hand over Aquitaine to the youngest brother, John, who had exploited the family feud to become his father's favourite. Richard could see no merit in losing a compelling asset in return for a pledge to a throne that he should be able to take himself. He (and secretly John) harried the ailing king into accepting their terms in 1189. He died two days later.

As must be evident, Henry was far more than an accomplice in the slaughter of an archbishop. He was a towering king. A 1968 film about him was entitled *A Lion in Winter*. He was a lion for all seasons.

Richard I (1189–99)

OVERRATED

Richard I was King of England; Duke of Normandy, Aquitaine and Gascony; Lord of Cyprus; Count of Anjou, Maine and Nantes; and the effective ruler of Brittany. He is one of only a very few English monarchs to be widely known by a positive nickname, 'the Lionheart' (which is much better than being dubbed 'the Unready', like Ethelred). He is probably the king with the highest level of recognition between William the Conqueror and Henry VIII. Surely, all this rendered him a great success story?

A strong counterargument exists to the contrary. That Richard was an exceptional soldier is hard to dispute (although his bravery could often be matched by a brutality which is striking even by the very uncompromising standards of his time). To be a good king is about more than being a great general.

Richard was not predestined for the collection of titles and accompanying lands that he would hold. He was born in England (it is thought near Oxford) in 1157. That a man who would become the King of England was actually born on its soil is a novelty during this period. He was, though, primarily raised in Poitiers. He was the third son to be born to Henry II and Eleanor of Aquitaine (technically the fourth, but their first son, William, had died at the age of 3 before Richard transpired).

As he was hardly at the top of the pecking order, he was not schooled to become a monarch. He appears to have been unusually interested in ideas, music and poetry. His main preoccupation was to become the master of the arts of war. In this he obviously excelled because at the age of 16 he was awarded the command of his own army. This was in the context of the Great Revolt of 1173 when, with the backing of his mother, brothers, Louis XIV of France and the King of Scotland, he took on his father for the future of the Crown. This early military enterprise proved to be a disaster. Henry II was, at this time, a savvier, smarter soldier than the rest of them. Richard had to plead for a pardon.

Richard's closest relationship was with his mother, Eleanor of Aquitaine. She was remarkable. There has been no other queen consort quite like her. She was at different moments the Queen of France and then of England. Aquitaine rendered her the wealthiest woman in Europe. She would outlive not only Henry II, from whom she became estranged, but four of her five sons. She was an inveterate fixer of dynastic marriages. She was an able administrator in her own right. She would turn up when Richard was travelling to the Crusades to dispense advice. She did not die until 1204, then aged 80. If she had lived a reasonably healthy life for another ten years, her last son, King John, might not have come as badly unstuck on multiple fronts as would prove to be his misfortune.

For most of his adult life, Richard had his sights set on acquiring his mother's domain in Aquitaine, not being the King of England. It was only when, first, his eldest brother Henry died (in 1183), then, second, his next brother Geoffrey also expired (1186) that a chance of seizing England and Aquitaine was open. When that opportunity arose, Richard was disinclined to share the spoils. This would be a major mistake.

Richard I (1189–99)

It is hard to appreciate the context of Richard's reign without examining three dimensions of it. The first is his intimate involvement in the Third Crusade (1189–92), which ultimately consumed half of his reign (it was not supposed to take that long, but his kidnapping extended his enforced absence). The second is his disagreements with his brother John, which would have a momentous effect on the administration of England when he was not there (the vast majority of his tenure). The final aspect is the somewhat bizarre nature of the bartering around his prospective marriage, which meant that he wed relatively late and would in death be childless. As a younger son, he started out with little influence over his own fate in this regard, only obtaining more authority over what he would do after he became king.

Richard and the Third Crusade are synonymous. He had been desperate to depart for the Holy Land since 1187 when the news of the fall of Jerusalem to Saladin and his Muslim troops reached Europe. It was impractical to mount such a long (and expensive) campaign while he and his father remained at loggerheads. If he were gone, his brother John, to whom Henry II had become close, was more than capable of intriguing to obtain the throne of England for himself.

Richard's coronation was thus the prelude to him leaving England for what in the best of conditions would be an atypically long adventure. Crusading cost a fortune. It would have been unwise to travel without the requisite resources and simply assume that plunder during passage would finance a large army. Henry II had left a sizeable surplus in the Treasury, but it would have to be supplemented somehow. Officeholders were compelled to pay to retain their berths, and other forms of extortion followed. It took several months for the cash required to be collected. Only then could the crusading be started.

In theory, this was a military expedition from western Europe of a scale never previously witnessed. Richard I and Philip II of France (although hardly all of France) had agreed to merge their efforts and take their forces along together. Whether this was out of mutual Christian devotion or because neither man trusted the other not to conspire against him if one, but not both, was away could be speculated upon. That their motives were not exclusively those of faith is suggested by the bargain at the outset that any lands taken during their invasion of the Middle East would be divided up equally.

There was meant to be a third member of this 'dream team', Frederick I, Holy Roman Emperor. He had indicated that he would be a full participant but died in 1190 before the venture got serious. His successor, Henry VI, promised his backing but prevaricated on delivering. He was able to exploit the vacuum of leadership left by Philip II and, even more effectively, the unavailability of Richard I.

To reach the Holy Land was a complicated combination of land and sea activity, adding to the cost. Richard and Philip decided to spend the winter months in Cyprus as the essentially uninvited guests of King Tancred. This proved to be sensitive as Richard was annoyed with his host because of the way in which he had treated his sister Joan, widow of the former King of Cyprus, who was owed money. The two men came to blows and it was Richard who, in a somewhat chaotic fashion, obtained Cyprus. This only led to more acrimony between himself and Philip II, Cyprus apparently not falling under the terms of the original accord to split spoils accumulated on a fifty-fifty basis. Philip was in any case not so pleased that Richard was continuing to stall on turning his engagement to Philip's sister Alice into any formal wedlock. Philip II and his men went on ahead. Christian unity was already being strained.

When Richard reached the Holy Land, he had victories but also encountered frustration. He went to Acre, which had been under siege from an early contingent of Crusaders since 1189 but was itself at risk of being encircled by a bigger Muslim army. Exhibiting his considerable military prowess, Richard broke the siege, secured control over the city and took more than 2,000 prisoners as his hostages. A different diplomatic disagreement then occurred but with Leopold of Austria, the surrogate for the Holy Roman Emperor, who expected to be seen as an equal but was not. Philip II headed for home.

Richard pressed on. With the prisoners of no particular value to him and a burden to take along to the next stop, he ordered them to be slaughtered (vicious even in the late twelfth century). He had another thumping victory at Arsuf to add to his reputation. He was closing in on Jerusalem. But he could not traverse further than Beit Nuba, a tantalising 12 miles from his target. The lie of the land, inclement weather and depleting stockpiles (he was the last king left in the field) meant that he had to settle for a three-year truce with Saladin, extract some tribute and start back to England. In that sense, the Third Crusade was a failure. Jerusalem would remain in the hands of an 'infidel'.

This was bad enough, but there was far worse to come. Richard's exit had been rushed and not well considered. He and a small band of his closest colleagues would be shipwrecked, captured and then handed over to Leopold of Austria, still smarting at Richard's reluctance to accord him a high status, who would then send him over to the Holy Roman Emperor. At this moment, any notion that shared Christian allegiance applied in high politics disappeared entirely. A ransom was placed on Richard. It was an eye-watering 150,000 silver marks, or about £100,000 in the exchange rates understood then (and an indescribable sum in today's money). No one had that sort of bounty immediately to hand. Richard would be a prisoner with no meaningful contact with his realm for more than an entire year. This would have been a crisis in any conditions. The domestic state of England made it more dire.

Richard's dysfunctional relations with his remaining brother John were critical to this situation.

The king had, in fairness, attempted to organise the affairs of his realms before the Crusade (and had not factored being incarcerated into those calculations). He did not want John to be his regent as he did not trust him at all. He had thus secured a pledge from his brother that he would not set foot in England for three years (the maximum time that Richard believed he would be away) and had named Arthur, his nephew by his deceased brother Geoffrey, then aged only 4, as his heir, and not John.

He did not cut out John completely. He was the Lord of Ireland (although his visit there in 1185 was not a success and the Pope refused to endorse him being crowned the king of that territory). He was appeased, or so Richard considered, by the grant of vast new lands, a lucrative Normandy province, the revenues from six English counties and the hand in marriage of Isabelle of Gloucester, an heiress.

With John seemingly satisfied, Richard left the administration of England to William Longchamp, to be assisted by Hugh de Puiset, the Bishop of Durham. Both were seen as safe pairs of hands.

The plan fell apart very quickly. In Cyprus, Eleanor of Aquitaine convinced Richard to cancel the three-year ban on John entering England. John would have disregarded it anyway and he had started to scheme against the two men supposed to safeguard the kingdom. However, while he was disruptive, he could not overthrow them. He lacked the support of the broader nobility to mount an insurrection. When rumours of John's misbehaviour were transmitted to Richard, Walter de Coutances, the highly regarded Archbishop of Rouen, was sent to inspect and intervene, and he threw his weight against John.

The aspiring king's position in France was weak. His mother was in charge of Aquitaine. Many of the other continental lands which he thought might fall to him in time preferred the minor Arthur as their eventual monarch. John became the junior partner of Philip II and sought conquests of his own, but he lost substantial terrain as a result of military miscalculation. He even tried a joint bid with Philip II to obtain the imprisoned

Richard from the Holy Roman Emperor and not for the best of motives. When Richard finally reached England in 1194, John had to make a grovelling plea to be pardoned. The king would spend most of the rest of his reign in France in a drive to make good John's losses.

There is a final twist in all this that mattered. Plan A for Richard's marriage had involved one of the daughters of Ramon Berenguer IV, the Count of Barcelona. As Henry II became more of a force in Europe, this scheme was abandoned in favour of an upgrade. In 1169, Plan B kicked in, with a treaty signed with Louis VII, which would involve Richard becoming engaged to Alice, one of his daughters. Two decades elapsed and the nuptials had not occurred, which increasingly irritated Philip. This was in part because Richard was disinterested and distracted (and perhaps not that into women anyway) but also because it was widely reported that Henry II had taken Alice, who was in his care, to be one of his (many) mistresses and, if certain stories are deemed accurate, had four illegitimate children by her. Father and son found it challenging enough to coexist without throwing in that aspect as well.

As was often seen, it was Eleanor of Aquitaine who provided Plan C for her favourite son. She visited Richard in Cyprus and brought with her Berengaria of Navarre as an alternative to the unwanted Alice. Navarre bordered Aquitaine to the south, so from Eleanor's perspective it was a sound match (even if it infuriated Philip II). Richard and Berengaria were married in Cyprus in some style. No child would materialise.

Professional Standing

How does one assess the professional standing of a monarch who spent only six months (if that) of his ten-year tenure as king in situ? An element of forgiveness can be shown for his initial long stretch abroad, in that the condition of Jerusalem was not a negligible question, the voyage to the Holy Land was more convoluted than it was reasonable to estimate and being kidnapped was not expected. Richard had known the risks that John would pose if inclined to meddle in English affairs and had sought to mitigate them. If after 1194 he had stayed in England, that would redeem him.

Yet he did not. He was home for about two months (March to May 1194) before departing back to France to restore his territories there and resume what was now a corrosive feud with Philip II. He would die before he could make a trip back to England. This time round, the charge that he was an absentee landlord is irresistible. What is more damning is that despite all that John had done (or tried and failed to do) in his own interests and against those of Richard and of his subjects, he was officially pronounced to be his brother's heir (with the young nephew Arthur demoted) and he was to remain in England, where it was close to certain that he would again be a political obstacle. This was at best a startling structure to leave behind. It can be condemned as awful leadership.

Richard simply had no concern whatsoever for the basics of domestic government in England. He did not take time to examine the structure of public administration, the actions of local authorities were a bore, and the law, which had been his father's mission, was neglected. He treated England as a kind of giant piggy bank to raid for his armed excursions (although the money soon ran out). It cannot even be asserted in his defence that he expended more affection and labour on the running of Aquitaine or Anjou. All his many territories served to fund the effort to secure new lands. This was less a polity than an embryonic form of pyramid scheme which came with shining armour.

His one saving grace is that the system of government which Henry II had left to his son was of a form that could not be totally destroyed by an absent king or a conniving prince of the realm. It endured, although it would be tested to its limits when John finally became king.

There was an element of luck in this institutional resilience, in that an outstanding man emerged who could keep the show on the road. Hubert Walter, Archbishop of Canterbury, had exceptional ability and managed to shield the country to some extent from what was otherwise stunning mismanagement. Richard's flair cannot spare him from the conclusion that any professional standing that he enjoyed was on the battlefield, and in every other respect he does not deserve a meritorious reputation.

Public Opinion

How the wider public evaluated a monarch who was not there is something of a mystery. Much of the subsequent popular division between 'Good King Richard', whose population ached to learn of his return to restore decency and order, and 'Bad Prince, then King, John', who cruelly undermined what should have been his brother's legacy, is a narrative shaped long after the event. It has been weaved into the folk story, which could be entirely fictional, around the deeds of Robin Hood (the Walt Disney cartoon of which has probably boosted Richard's image). The high taxes of Richard's tenure, which will be referred to shortly, would have been disliked quite intensely.

The counterbalance is that the Church, at least to begin with, was an advocate for the Crusades, and although accounts of Richard's triumphs at arms would have taken many months to come back from the Middle East and then be recounted into towns and villages, the impression left would have been of a warrior king like none before. That must have had an impact.

It is far less probable that his departure to France (with John better placed to seek to pull the strings) would have been greeted with the same degree of approving admiration. This was all too familiar. Although Henry II had put a solid structure in place that cushioned the blow, Richard did not care for this.

Financial Competence

Richard's military masterplans were reckless and ruinous in terms of expenditure. He would fleece the English at all levels not once, but twice (albeit that the second occasion was not deliberate). His father had been an extremely rich monarch and by innovations in tax collection had remained solvent. He would hand over an enchanting financial situation to the son who replaced him. It did not last long.

As set out previously, the reserves were decimated at the outset of Richard's reign to put down a suitable deposit on the Third Crusade, to which he was committed. Even this was not enough, so those who had offices were charged to keep them. The most rational means to recoup those fees would be corruption and self-enrichment while the king was hundreds of miles away with his army. Every tier of society would find themselves to some extent subsidising a crusade, which eventually fell short.

The capture of Richard I, and the ransom note which was circulated thereafter, was a massive fiscal hit for a country that had already taken a pummelling. The amount that Henry VI demanded to release Richard from his (silver, not iron) chains was staggering. At 150,000 silver marks (or around £100,000) it was more than double the total sum of annual royal income for the throne of England.

What followed was rather more extensive than a whip-round among friends for a respectable cause. It took all the imagination (and some veiled threats) from Archbishop Walter to launch the appeal. Officeholders were once more to be invoiced for remaining in position (and once more would be well inclined to recoup that charge by undesirable and illicit means). All knights found that they were expected to hand over 20 shillings (a cost which they also probably delegated to others). The whole output of wool controlled by the Cistercian monks was forcibly requisitioned for the cause. Some Church treasures were brusquely seized. A ransom chest duly appeared in St Paul's Cathedral.

It was close to a miracle that this flabbergasting amount of money was raised in under one year. The effect on the economy must have been devastating. To cap it all, Richard when released then spent a tidy amount on holding a second coronation before disappearing on an expensive military exercise. His tenure would be one long pursuit of gain and glory to be paid for by his subjects.

Foreign Policy

It is challenging to distinguish between the Third Crusade and the subsequent storming into France and any sense of a foreign policy of wider scope or strategy. Richard was not much intrigued by Scotland (which was comparatively quiet), Wales (hardly a trophy to him), or Ireland (other than imposing his brother on it as lord, which appeared to unite the otherwise divided clans in deeply disapproving of him personally). Not just England but the British Isles did not cut the mustard.

Any balanced cost–benefit analysis of the Third Crusade would have to conclude that it was not worth it. What spoils were won were insignificant when contrasted with the expense of blood and money required, all of which could not displace Saladin from Jerusalem. The mission served to make the animosity felt between the monarchs of western Europe more dangerous than before it started. There was a reason why, when the Fourth Crusade (1202–04) was mooted, many steered clear.

In purely military terms, Richard's intervention in France from 1194 to 1199 can be viewed as a success in that much of what John had managed to throw away was snatched back by force for England. This was not, however, achieved cheaply, and once Richard had died, needlessly exposing himself to risk yet again, it would not take John long to lose what had been regained and much more besides.

There was no other vision in this foreign policy. Henry II had looked with interest across much more of Europe and pondered how he could turn his position into a profit without sustaining a high cost. Diplomacy was not Richard's strong suit. What is more, what could have been cards for him to play if he had turned his mind that way, children to marry off to assist the dynasty, were not there.

Succession

That Richard had no issue would become an issue for England. There were very few options available. John had been reinstated as heir, despite his double-dealing, in 1194. Richard does not seem to have evaluated the merits of returning to Arthur of Brittany as an alternative (Arthur would meet his end once John was king, captured and murdered at Poitou, conceivably at the king's own hand). None of this would have been needed if Richard himself had married earlier, or even later had produced a son.

This does not appear to have mattered to him. The soap opera around Richard's twenty-year engagement to Alice of France, and her supposed intimacy with his father (she did show that she was fertile) is such that it is comprehensible that she had ceased to be the optimal bride, irrespective of what Philip II may have asserted. Yet as Richard rose up the ranks and came closer to the throne, he was in a place where he could have renounced that marriage agreement for another and sought an heir.

The desire not to annoy Philip II by taking such a step looks feeble. There were other female relatives of the French king who could have been seconded if keeping him amiable was so vital (it is not at all evident that it was). Once Richard was wed, bounced into it by a mother who thoroughly understood the need for heirs and several spares, he saw his wife about as often as he stared out at England. The ramifications would be huge. It doomed the country after his death. It was a full dereliction of duty.

Richard instead left behind John, who would take on the Church at home (being excommunicated for his intrigues), be deprived of Normandy, almost lose the country to an invasion from France, annoy the barons so much that they would force him to accept Magna Carta restricting royal authority, and die with a baby son (Henry III), with all the insecurity that comes from a regency. None of this was Richard's fault as such, but it could have been avoided. He is an overrated monarch.

Edward III (1327–77)

UNDERRATED

A reign of fifty years in length might be expected to establish the name of that monarch forcefully in national memory. Indeed, at the time, the duration of Edward III on the throne was the longest since Henry III (1216–72) and he would hold that record until George III (1760–1820), although for more than two decades that king suffered from periodic bursts of insanity and for his last nine years he lived in miserable conditions while his eldest son acted as prince regent. Edward III would slow with age and make mistakes (long reigns do not tend to be associated with the happiest of endings), but his mind would remain intact even if the glories of his earlier period as king fast faded in the memory.

Yet, although the fifth longest-serving sovereign after Elizabeth II, Victoria, George III and Henry III (with James I putting in a shift of almost sixty years as James VI of Scotland), Edward III would rarely be on the tip of the tongue when discussing medieval monarchy. It is more probable that Edward I (1272–1307), the 'Hammer of the Scots', would be recalled, and he was certainly a larger-than-life figure who is appropriately regarded as an unusually significant king (not overrated or underrated). In many respects Edward III was at least as substantial a figure as him, but that is not often conceded. His name is lost in the sweeping summary of the Hundred Years' War, which in a sense he initiated but made a tactical repositioning from after just over twenty years, with no plans to continue the conflict.

Whatever the reason, the reign and reputation of Edward III are in need of some rehabilitation. He was as successful a warrior as other better-remembered monarchs of these times, had a more sweeping impact on society as a whole than others, whose triumphs were invariably and solely due to combat, was confronted with a crisis in the form of the Black Death, which placed the survival of the people in peril (as it did throughout Europe but with a particular menace in England) and fathered no fewer than thirteen children in wedlock. Ironically, however, this did not mean that he could avert succession difficulties.

This is clearly a king who would have a disproportionate impact on his realm and one whose better points significantly outnumber the arguments that can be mobilised against him. This is even more impressive when it is retold how exposed a position he was in when he began his tenure. There are three features of his time as king which are seminal to an appreciation of why he deserves a better rating than some historians have offered him, and certainly more of a profile than he presently enjoys. These are the desperate nature of his inheritance, the opening shots of what would later be called the Hundred Years' War and the shock to the economy and social order of the Black Death, an occurrence with little parallel and minimal means in terms of known medicine to combat it.

Edward I had been succeeded, relatively peacefully, by Edward II, whom he had made the first Prince of Wales after completing the outright subjugation of that territory. If there were to be a competition for the worst, rather than best, King of England, then Edward II could throw his crown into the ring. Almost everything that his father had achieved was lost. The administration and reputation of the Crown had fallen into disrepair and civil insurrection was becoming the norm within England.

The full charge sheet against Edward II is comprehensive. He was inclined towards unpopular male favourites – Piers Gaveston and Hugh Despenser the Younger – with the strong hint of sexual desire being at the core of their appeal to him. This led to the Ordinances of 1311 (a mere four years into his reign) which involved restrictions on his power. Gaveston was murdered at the behest of nobles not long after. Edward's conduct of the war with Scotland was inept in the extreme, which allowed Robert the Bruce to turns the tables on England. He then set upon the idea of enhancing his armed might (such as it was) by compelling common people to leave the land and fight unpaid on his behalf. This was not a vote winner. He was no more effective in France than he had been north of the border.

As a result, Edward II found himself to blame when the Great Famine of 1315–17 struck England (it was a terrible force over much of northern Europe). Although in essence this was nothing to do with him, since abnormal weather conditions destroyed crops and caused the price of food to double in a few weeks, the sense of maladministration under him that had already become widespread would deepen. It is not certain how many people died of hunger, but the lower end of estimates is 10 per cent of the population.

Edward II was also the cause of fratricide within the court and a breakdown with his parliaments. He had his cousin, Thomas, Earl of Lancaster, executed on risible charges in 1322, which made lesser nobles wonder whether anyone was safe from arbitrary removal. He then fell out with his wife, Isabella of France, repossessing her estates, dismissing her retinue and humiliating her in public. When called upon to pay homage to the King of France, he considered the engagement too risky to undertake himself, so he sent his son – the future Edward III – at the age of 11 to do this for him. In retrospect, as he was inviting an uprising against him, the only surprise is that it did not come sooner (although there had been a rehearsal revolt in 1322 aimed against the influence of Hugh Despenser).

When it did come, it was spectacular. Edward II's own queen led the charge in the company of Roger Mortimer, a senior nobleman, but not of the very highest rank, who was an opportunist and had become the queen's lover. Once they had set out their stall, the die was cast. Edward could find nobody to assist him, and he was captured, imprisoned, forced to renounce the throne, and killed (there is a lively historical deliberation as to exactly how gruesome the end method deployed to dispose of him was). Edward, then the Prince of Wales, was party to these proceedings against his father, courtesy of his mother, and was crowned king in their aftermath, but at the tender age of 14 and not yet his own man. This was bad enough, but Mortimer was acting like his regent and had eyes on the throne himself.

Without some courage and cunning there was a chance that Edward III would suffer the sort of fate that Edward V would do a tad over 150 years later. Mortimer had not taken long to find an excuse to send Edmund, Duke of Kent, the younger brother of the deposed king, to meet his maker. Wisely, the new king did not wait to see what might happen next. He intervened directly to ensure that Mortimer was seized, put on trial and then executed. He brought his mother back into the fold and was forgiving towards those who had backed Mortimer previously – all this before reaching the age of 18. He would mostly take care to keep the nobility loyal and content by an adopting an inclusive approach towards them.

While Edward was (effectively) securing his throne, action elsewhere created a chance for him to look to obtain another. Charles IV of France had died childless in 1328. As Edward was the son of his sister (Isabella) and the most logical nephew to follow him on conventional bloodline calculations (but this was not always accepted as the means to decide succession), he had a strong argument in his favour. This was tacitly conceded in Paris,

Edward III (1327–77)

but the idea of handing over France lock, stock and barrel to the Plantagenet dynasty in this fashion had little charm to the French nobility or to its (generally weak) parliament. The powers that be decided to retire the Capetian family (who had run out of options) and switch to Philip VI of Valois, who was only a cousin of the deceased Charles IV (not as close to him as Edward III) but appeared the consensus candidate. In 1328, Edward was scarcely King of England and with a totally unreliable 'Protector' in the form of Mortimer to contend with, so he did not press his claim as forcefully as he might have done if he had been older and in a stronger situation. He bided his time and agreed to cross the Channel to pay his homage to Philip VI in 1331 (the assumption had long been that the King of England ranked second to the King of France even at times when, such as with Henry II, the ruler of England also had lands which constituted the majority of French soil). The occasion ran smoothly enough but had its difficult moments. It was the last time homage was paid.

A military entanglement was averted for the moment. Edward had issues aplenty on his plate as he sought to restore order and widespread respect for the Crown, which had evaporated under his father. He concentrated on the fundamentals, seeking out a wife and starting off a family of heirs (which is more than Richard I, for all his skill in combat, ever managed to focus on). He was married to Philippa d'Hainault, a very shrewd selection in that she was one step distant from the intrigues of France, was intelligent and a sound source of advice, was capable of serving well as his regent when he was away and would be the mother of no fewer than thirteen children (only the wife of George III would produce more). The first of these was Edward, later known as the Black Prince, who was born in 1330 – with the king not yet at his eighteenth birthday, succession thinking began admirably early in his tenure.

The force of Edward's claim to France was, nonetheless, a running sore. He was bound to scratch it. When he did, it would be the essence of his foreign policy and would draw England as a whole into it. However, he was not impetuous. It would be 1340 before he cleared the decks and declared himself King of France. That would prove momentous, but his campaign to impose his authority would also have to be suspended for a while in the late 1340s.

There was an unavoidable break in proceedings courtesy of the Black Death. It had come out of Asia slowly and arrived in continental Europe. It is thought that it entered England through a sailor who had arrived from Gascony in June 1348. The plague would spread from the south-west of England (Bristol was decimated), up through much of the rest of the country, spread to Dublin and into Ireland, move on relentlessly to Wales and march apace into Scotland. In around 500 days, it had managed to establish itself throughout the British Isles, bar the most isolated places.

Devastating is scarcely the word for it. As we do not know with confidence what the population of England was then, it is challenging to estimate what percentage of the population died at its hands. The absolute floor is 25 per cent. The more recent ceiling of evaluations is closer to 60 per cent. It would be no shock at all if it were in the region of 50 per cent. These are all astounding statistics. It had a massive social effect on the country. The most instant was that there was an extraordinary shortage of labour on farms (peasants were less capable of hiding themselves from the Black Death than their lords were), which meant wage inflation, price inflation and the chance that famine would follow the plague.

The measures that the king and Parliament could take were extremely limited. Vaccines, of course, were not a possibility. The short-term response was an Ordinance of Labourers in 1349 and another in 1351, which was a crude but not entirely inefficient attempt to control costs and impose social stability.

The Black Death was a shock for which the twenty-first century, never mind the fourteenth, would not have been prepared.

Historians have, nevertheless, been inclined to concur that its aftermath was managed rather better in England than elsewhere (certainly than in France where society imploded).

Taking all this into account, Edward III should be assessed according to the measures of monarchy.

Professional Standing

Until the very last few years of his reign, when age and what was seen as an upstart very young mistress led his reputation to be devalued, Edward had a high professional standing. He sought conciliation with the nobility and would use marriages to his vast collection of children to bind them closer. He invented a new rank of nobility when he made his eldest son the first Duke of Cornwall. Other sons would take variants on that title as well. He would promote other nobles to become earls. His court was the centre of pomp and pageantry, and enticing for the nobility to be part of. He took on chivalry as a cause, re-enacting the roundtable of Arthurian legend in 1344 and founding the Order of the Garter four years later. The message to his contemporaries was clear. This was a tent to be inside.

Edward also sought a far more harmonious relationship with his parliaments. This was generally achieved, but he learnt lessons from one serious error when, in a fit of pique, he unilaterally dismissed the sheriffs only to have the House of Commons express its disapproval loudly. A gracious U-turn was witnessed. By taking a less confrontational attitude, he made Parliament a partner rather than a rival or enemy. This allowed him to press for regular increases in taxation without triggering significant rancour.

Another institution which received kindly attention was the Church. This was in a poor state at the start of Edward's reign due to the weakness of the papacy, where schism had led to rival

Popes declaring that they were the mouthpiece of the Almighty in Avignon and Rome. This inhibited appointments. The clergy would also suffer desperately later in Edward's tenure because of heavy losses in the Black Death.

The king was also an advocate of legal reform. He managed to convince Parliament to accept the Treason Act of 1351 (what was treason up until this legislation was often unappealingly arbitrary). The network of justices of the peace was enhanced and what fell under their scope was expanded. Most of the time, Edward chose his senior courtiers well, the last one of note being William of Wykeham.

In an immensely important cultural development, Edward pushed the English language in official circles. It would also become the language of the law and heard within courts on a more frequent basis (the main device for this was the Statute of Pleading, 1362). The administration of justice was stronger for proceedings which could be understood by a wider range of people. This is an admirable record. If Edward had died in 1372, then it would have been unblemished, but the visibility of Alice Perrers, a malign mistress, and the feeling that he had lost his grip, led the 'Good Parliament' of 1376 to attack and admonish him. Perhaps mercifully, he died in 1377, so had not undone all the good beforehand.

Public Opinion

Historians agree that Edward obtained a virtually unprecedented popularity at the start of his reign, and despite bouts of heavy taxation, time spent abroad and the Black Death did not lose favour throughout his tenure. When he did, it was often put down to rogue advisers and not the king himself. That might have been a charitable assessment, but Edward would not have corrected it.

Edward III (1327–77)

The reasons why he was held in high esteem are several. It began with not being his father. He was seen as having brought back order after two decades when the country teetered on the brink of chaos. He suffered no revolt of any scale during his tenure, which is rare indeed over a fifty-year period.

His standing among what could be labelled the middle to lesser elites was buttressed by a major reform which he implemented in military matters. The old forms of feudalism were sidelined. A contractual understanding was introduced into the army. Captains would be compensated for their service (often paid, it should be observed, by the proceeds of plunder), and this was seen as a considerable improvement on what had gone before, and it was sugar-coated with chivalry.

Edward actively wanted to be popular. He was an instinctive showman. Wherever he went, the poor would obtain some benefit from his presence. Aware that warfare was not always regarded well if it cost too much, he had reports issued from the front in the name of himself or of his commanders. It was propaganda, to be sure, but it demystified to a degree what he was striving to achieve in France. Although Edward's standing was lower at the end of his reign, it held its own to an impressive extent for fifty years.

Financial Competence

In contrast to other aspects of Edward's reign, fiscal coherence started badly but improved a lot over time. The royal treasury was in a woeful state when Edward II's tenure as king was abruptly terminated. It would take some time to restore it to a satisfactory position and that would necessitate taxation.

This process was not over by the moment that Edward determined to pursue his claim to France, and he was dependent on Italian bankers and other financiers to a destabilising degree. In

1340, he was in a dire financial position. He had to reform the administration of collecting taxes and hike them yet again to balance the books and swerve a cash-flow cul-de-sac. He needed to impose fiscal rules upon himself and to adopt controls which would allow his aspirations in France to be self-sustaining. These included sweeping reforms of the coinage in 1344 with gold coins produced for the first time. Later on, having captured the French king, John II, and taken him to England, he should have hit the jackpot when in 1360 France agreed to pay a fantastic 3 million crowns for his release. Alas, raising that vast sum of money proved to be utterly impossible and John would die in England in 1364. By then, however, various reforms and the practice of outsourcing tax increases to his territories within France (even if that prompted resentment which would come back to inconvenience him) meant fiscal stability.

The king (and the queen, who probably understood the clockwork of the market better than most) were extremely insightful when it came to commerce and trade. England had become a powerhouse in the supply of wool – according to a recent and persuasive book,[3] this was due to the elimination of wolves in the country by 1290. But it had not appreciated how to maximise money from this position. Edward took a profound interest in how pricing for wool functioned in Flanders, which dominated the trade, and succeeded in sharply increasing the price of wool at no revenue loss (indeed substantial gain). England would become rich from the wool trade.

Foreign Policy

The story of foreign policy under Edward III is largely one about France, but not as exclusively as would be true for other English

---

3   Robert Winder, *The Last Wolf: The Hidden Springs of Englishness* (2017).

monarchs during the Plantagenet era. He had thrown down the gauntlet in 1340 by insisting that he, not Philip VI, was the rightful king in Paris. He had a grand success at the naval battle at Sluys in that year, in which the French fleet, which was not huge to begin with, suffered severe losses. This meant that for decades to come, the chance of an invasion from the other side of the Channel was extremely slim. The war would not be extended to English soil. Edward also established the first formal administration for his fleet, and the Royal Navy would be built on it.

There then came an annoying period of stalemate. Edward piled resources into France, but Philip VI would not come out and fight, so no decisive encounter could be scheduled which would allow Edward to enter Paris and demand a coronation. This was rational from Philip's point of view. It caused far more distress to his rival. It looked as if Edward would have to pack up and move home.

The breakthrough started with Henry of Derby finally making an advance of some substance. A dramatic encounter took place at Crécy in 1346. An English army was outnumbered to a considerable extent but secured the superior spot for combat. A French army was obliterated, and from then on, the House of Valois was on the defensive. A further stunning victory would take place at Poitiers in 1356 with Edward's son and heir apparent, the Black Prince, in the vanguard. The French king fell into English hands. A protracted round of negotiations about his fate took place, and a settlement was reached which reflected that the balance of power on the ground had shifted.

The accord that emerged was the Treaty of Brétigny in 1360. Considering how many high cards he held, Edward III was magnanimous in victory. He received Aquitaine and Calais back and was pledged an absolute fortune of a ransom for John II (which, as set out above, sadly failed to be deposited). In return, he withdrew his claim to be King of France. If that had been the end of it, then it would have been a twenty-year war not a Hundred

Years' War, but France recovered once Charles V became its king, a further outbreak of plague meant mutual disengagement and Edward faltered as he aged. In the hour of his death, the amount of terrain that he actively controlled in France had again eroded.

France was not the only element of foreign policy that mattered. Under Edward III, English authority over Scotland would become far more potent. At the outset of his reign, the very young Edward had in 1328 felt the need to agree the Treaty of Northampton which acknowledged his father's losses. He would later through his armies come good at the siege of Berwick, see a triumph at the Battle of Halidon Hill, play off rival contenders to the Scottish throne to satisfactory effect, and lure King David II into an ill-advised skirmish at Neville's Cross, which meant the Scottish monarch (his brother-in-law, thanks to his marriage to Edward's sister Joan) became his captive.

A last item of value, as it shows some foresight: Edward would conclude the Anglo-Portuguese Treaty of 1373, part of a process taken further by the Treaty of Windsor in 1386 for a long-lasting alliance.

Succession

One might have thought that, having produced thirteen children, succession would not have been a worry for Edward III. That would have been true if Edward, the Black Prince, a man with a military reputation that eclipsed even his father, had not predeceased him in 1376, meaning that a 9-year-old boy, then Prince Richard, would be his heir. Edward's second son, Lionel, Duke of Clarence, had also died earlier in 1368. There was, potentially menacingly, a third son, John of Gaunt, Duke of Lancaster, who was very much alive and kicking, and was thought by many to consider himself the best choice as king. There was also a fourth son, Edward, Duke of York, who would outlive him for many years (until 1402).

His ambitions would be contained for the time being. It could be asserted that it might have been better for England if they had not been, because the hapless Richard II would turn out to have too much of Edward II's DNA and would meet a similar end in 1399. Yet Edward III had signalled that Richard would be his heir, which in the end would be enough to overcome doubt and let him be seated upon the throne.

Edward made one more decision about the succession which would send shockwaves later. He did not include the solitary daughter of Lionel, Philippa, and her potential children in his considerations. The struggle over the succession would hence be between the descendants of the Duke of Lancaster and the Duke of York. Edward, who wanted a united kingdom with such passion, would actually undermine it. Without a crystal ball, however, this could not be divined. It does not stop him being an underrated monarch.

Henry V (1413–22)

OVERRATED

When you have William Shakespeare and Laurence Olivier as friends, who cares about enemies? The combination of one of the most memorable scenes in the Bard's plays and a 1944 film designed to boost morale on the home front have framed Henry V's reputation (although a story which may have reminded those in cinemas that France, not Germany, had been their country's historic foe might be deemed a curious choice). Henry was the ultimate warrior king, a military genius who led from the front, with the welfare of those under his command always in his mind. He was tall, handsome, articulate and cultured, not merely an exceptionally capable soldier. That he died young (aged 35) adds to the spectacle and the story. Taken before the moment of his supreme triumph, mere weeks before he would have been crowned the King of France as well as England, his tale is tinged with tragedy. If only he had perished while valiantly prosecuting a campaign, rather than from the more mundane illness which actually took his life (dysentery probably, although there are those who have put forward smallpox, or even leprosy), he would have been John F. Kennedy with a lance.

It is a compelling, even spell-binding, discourse. It has seized the English imagination for centuries. The assumption, implicitly, is that what was glory for Henry V personally was good for his subjects. That there were costs which flowed from his lust for conquest is rarely factored into the equation. There is also a built-in, if subconscious, deduction that if he had recovered from whatever struck him down, (a) he would have been both King of England and King of France, (b) he could have retained the throne of France without consistent revolts against his rule, and (c) England would have benefited from this.

A more rounded view of this fascinating but flawed monarchy is required. It is hard to see past the image to consider the reality more circumspectly. Henry V was not a bad king (if one destined to have a short reign), but he has a lot more in common with Richard I than with the likes of Henry VII. If being the champion of war and highly effective in combat is accepted as the currency of kingship, at least in the fourteenth and fifteenth centuries, then Henry should be saluted as standing in the first rank of monarchs. If the criteria for considering him are broader and more sophisticated than that, then he should not.

Henry was a dynamic and restless figure. He was also the product of his very turbulent times. To acquire a full sense of him requires an appreciation of his setting. This involves the complicated circumstances and interconnections which link Richard II to his father Henry IV and to Henry himself. It is compounded by the political situation in France in the first two decades after Richard II, where the manifest madness of Charles VI had created internal strife on a scale to encourage the English, who had largely been dormant on French territory for more than three decades, that they should reignite the Hundred Years' War. Finally, there is the need to remember that the Battle of Agincourt was about more than the outstanding performance of the English with their longbows, but also involved some distasteful punishment meted out to enemies, part of a pattern of brutality from Henry V that was a departure even from the norms of his era, never mind modern expectations. If he is to be hailed as a regional version of Alexander the Great, then he also had aspects of a regional Vlad the Impaler too.

When Henry was born in Monmouth Castle in 1386, he was far from a king-in-waiting. His father, Henry Bolingbroke, the Earl of Derby, was the eldest son of John of Gaunt, Duke of Lancaster, who was the third son of Edward III and still very much an active participant on the political scene, not always on the same side as his son. Henry Bolingbroke was part of the intrigue at court regarding his cousin Richard II, grandson of Edward III and son of Edward, the Black Prince, who had assumed the throne at the age of 10 in 1377, almost a decade before the young Henry was born. From the outset there had been those who disputed either his right to succeed (although that was hard to do) or his qualities as a monarch (a more straightforward line of argument). Henry Bolingbroke appears to have been at least aware of the revolts of the Lords Appellant against the king in 1388, and a sympathiser, but he managed to emerge from that fracas with his head in place and later became the Duke of Hereford.

This comparative harmony did not last very long. Sniping at Richard II was a regular occurrence. He was viewed as weak, took poor counsel and remained childless. Henry Bolingbroke almost certainly held that view but would not move overtly against the king without his father's clear consent, which was not forthcoming. He settled instead on scheming. This cannot have been especially subtle as Richard (not the sharpest tool in the box) spotted this and banished him abroad, initially for ten years, later reduced, not quite on appeal, to six years. John of Gaunt did not object to this sanction.

It was the death of his father in February 1399 that unleashed a chain of events ending in usurpation. Richard increased the sentence on Henry Bolingbroke to banishment for life, vetoed his elevation to the Duchy of Lancaster and then headed off on a mission to Ireland. A twist in all this is that the young Henry of Monmouth was not with his father abroad, but in the care of and a ward of Richard, who appears to have looked after him well and took him along on his visit to Ireland as part of a sizeable entourage.

Perhaps too sizeable. Henry Bolingbroke made the most of Richard being out of England to arrive there himself, supposedly to reassert his inheritance as Duke of Lancaster, but when it became plain that a bigger prize was there for the taking, to launch an all-out coup d'état. Richard hurried back from Ireland with a small fighting force, only to discover that the numbers who would rally to him were minimal. He had little choice but to surrender to Bolingbroke, who had himself crowned and Richard imprisoned. The ex-king was compelled to abdicate, citing his own unworthiness to serve, and died in February 1400 (plausibly of involuntary starvation). The junior Henry returned to England as the new heir to the throne, his father having sidelined the 7-year-old Earl of March whom Richard had picked as heir.

A son forcing his father out as king for his ineptitude or infirmity (as Edward III did with Edward II, albeit with others really overseeing the deed) is one thing. A cousin with a decent but not dominant blood claim on the throne, removing a king and then being associated with his demise, was another. The means by which Henry IV had made himself king, and thus rendered his son the Prince of Wales, would always be controversial. There was an immediate conspiracy in 1400 which was suppressed. A far more serious menace arrived in the alliance of the Percy family with Owen Glendower, leading to a battle fought at Shrewsbury in 1403, in which the younger Henry was a significant feature in a clear victory. 'Prince Hal', as Shakespeare referred to him in *Henry IV, Part One*, was struck in the face by an arrow, a wound which in the vast majority of cases would have been fatal, but an adept medical man kept him alive.

Henry V (1413–22)

There would be more rumblings of discontent throughout Henry IV's tenure. To cope with this, he adopted a more collegiate style of government than his predecessors. His Council became a true decision-making body, with his key allies in the nobility and his political fixer, Thomas Arundel, the Archbishop of Canterbury, as his agent. The king was, though, from 1408 onwards, inflicted by a mysterious illness (leprosy has often been suggested), which physically disfigured him and would lead to prolonged absence from the affairs of state (some whispered, perhaps with the Prince of Wales in assent, that abdication should be implemented). During this period, the future Henry V took the helm and eased out Archbishop Arundel, but when his father was able to come back to meetings, he put Henry back in his box, and the archbishop was restored as a leading light of the court and kingdom.

This did not mark a breach between father and son, although Henry IV may have found the Prince of Wales's impatience to take the reins galling. After all, if he had not gambled with his fate in 1399, his offspring would not have had the opportunity to assume the throne. Henry was, nonetheless, at his father's side when he died in 1413 and had the status and training to become king in his wake.

One of the areas where father and son had disagreed in Council was France. England had not been much involved there for many years. Diplomatic ties had been strained with the removal of Richard II because Henry IV had sent back Richard's second wife, Isabella, who had been married to him at the age of 6 (so becoming England's youngest queen consort), but without her valuable collection of jewels.

Matters had moved on from this. There was now a new opening. The sitting French king, Charles VI, was vulnerable to bouts of extreme insanity (including, allegedly, thinking that he was made of glass) and there were concerns about the fitness of his son, the Dauphin Charles, to rule as well. Not only the day-to-day authority of the monarch but the longer-term viability of the existing line was disputed.

The competing aspirants were the Duke of Orléans (the brother of the king but with his mental facilities intact) and the Duke of Burgundy (the cousin of the afflicted monarch). With Henry IV sufficiently settled as king, the English had the incentive and the resources with which to meddle.

The difficulty was that father and son had different allies in mind. Henry IV liked the Orléans faction (who came to be regarded as the Armagnacs). The Prince of Wales went with the Burgundy lobby. This could lead to farcical scenes depending on whether the king was well enough to attend Council. When the younger Henry was in command, an expedition was sent out to aid the Burgundian army, but it had to return when Henry IV raised himself from his sickbed. In a total reversal, Prince Thomas, Duke of Clarence, the second son of Henry IV, was ordered to set off with an impressive fleet to assist the Duke of Orléans. The Prince of Wales refused to travel with him and was accused of disloyalty.

It is important to note what Henry IV did not do, despite becoming re-engaged in French high politics. He did not insist that he (and after him, his eldest son) was the legitimate monarch of France (or an heir to the existing king as second best) on the basis of Edward III's not unreasonable claim to this. In so far as Henry IV had a plan here, it would appear to have been to back the eventual winner in the tussle for the French throne and be rewarded with lands lost in the last years of Edward III. He did not want to re-engage England with France on a semi-permanent basis. It was a pragmatic plot. Nor, as far as we can tell, did the Prince of Wales think that he could be the credible King of France. He was also backing his adopted colleagues – the Duke of Burgundy and his troops – for bounty. This would remain the position until he had acquired the English Crown in 1413 and not evolve until the Battle of Agincourt.

Henry V (1413–22)

Agincourt would prove an unanticipated bonanza for the new king. It was almost his undoing. He had marched his troops (already depleted by hunger and disease) some 260 miles in less than three weeks towards Calais. It was a risky, even reckless, decision. He and his men could easily have been cornered and killed, placing the English monarchy itself in peril. Instead, it was the French who were to bring catastrophe on themselves. Although they outnumbered the English by a hefty margin, they picked the wrong place to mount a full-scale battle. The longbows ruled the day as arrows rained on the French forces and those knights who moved forward found themselves in thick mud, unable to wield their swords and hacked to death by the English. The cream of the French military was lost in three hours. Any chance they had of regrouping later was reduced substantially when Henry had a huge number of prisoners (probably more in total than the captors holding them) slaughtered. This was, alas, one of a number of instances of his callous cruelty, seen in England as well as within France (deliberately having women and children seeking sanctuary from the siege of Rouen of 1417 isolated so that they starved to death was the worst incident). Henry could now target the French title. The Duke of Burgundy was in his pocket. The Duke of Orléans would be killed by his acolytes in 1419. By the Treaty of Troyes (1420), Henry was to marry Catherine of Valois and become heir to the throne.

The pursuit of absolute victory in France therefore became the essence of Henry V's reign. How does he rate against five measures of monarchy?

Professional Standing

Henry V certainly had a honeymoon period as the new monarch. He had served an apprenticeship as a leading figure at Council (almost a regent when his father was very sickly), even if Henry IV ended that arrangement once he was well enough to do so. He had a less tetchy dialogue with Parliament as well. A very small movement against him in 1413 did not attract support. He was secure as king.

He made his standing stronger still by initial magnanimity. He had the remains of Richard II reburied in Westminster Abbey. He allowed those who had supported that king to have their titles back. He was well disposed towards other noble families who had fallen out with his father. The Earl of March, a theoretical alternative to him as Richard II had anointed him his heir, was in no danger of a one-way ticket to the Tower of London as long as he retained his fidelity to him (which he consistently did). There was a sense of reconciliation, of what had been a usurpation becoming part of the furniture.

The contest within the ruling family did have a draining effect on their overall authority. Henry was obliged in 1414 to acknowledge the increasing salience of the House of Commons by conceding that while he could accept or reject a bill put before him, he was not allowed to amend it as he saw fit.

His exalted position meant that despite this, Parliament was essentially sympathetic to his ambitions. The House of Commons would vote him a double subsidy in advance of his trek to France in 1415 (in part because they thought that he would recapture land and wealth that would then finance him). It was an era of good feeling. His astonishing achievement at Agincourt would be hailed by his peers.

The love affair would not, however, continue indefinitely. His harsh pursuit of the Lollards (religious dissenters) in 1414–15 raised eyebrows. His insistence that the sentence awarded in 1417 to Sir John Oldcastle, who had been close to Henry IV – when he had been found guilty, on a dubious basis, of plotting against the king – should be death by burning was contentious. He won favour by pressing the use of English: this section of the Plantagenets, with his father doing so first, used English as its mother tongue. But he was not much taken by royal administration, local government, the judiciary or the health of the Church of England. He did not seek out able men to act on his behalf in these areas either. It was warfare and little else.

That would erode his professional standing before his premature death. Parliament and Council grew anxious about his absences. He was not in France for very long in 1415, coming back to get the plaudits due to him, but also because of practicalities such as restocking his resources and deciding on his next gambit, and he remained in England for the better part of eighteen months. When he left again for France, he would not be seen again at or near Westminster for three and a half years, hurtling home to be at the coronation of Catherine of Valois as queen, before making more tracks for France. Arrangements during his time away were haphazard. Richard I had been abroad for longer, but he had been bound for the Holy Land and had then found himself imprisoned. Henry could almost have commuted if he had wanted. His professional standing was still positive at the time of his death but with a downwards trajectory.

Public Opinion

Henry was popular at the time of his accession. He was a more open and charismatic figure than his father. That his coronation took place in the midst of an exceptional snowstorm (in the month of April) struck some of a superstitious disposition as a warning. Most, however, backed him with vigour. The harsh handling of the Lollards suggested that there was scant room for dissent under his tenure.

His victory at Agincourt seems to have triggered sincere and sustained celebration. Success (and also failure) in combat was often seen as an indication of God's approval (or not) of a monarch. While he continued to cover himself in glory, the mass public, in so far as they concentrated on these events, were likely to see him as a heroic individual. His death was almost certainly greeted with real sorrow.

Financial Competence

Neither Henry IV nor Henry V had a mastery of money. The old king had been through a total of ten treasurers in thirteen years, and they had sought to improve his finances. But they could not do so without a lot more revenue from the nobility, which Henry IV calculated would be more trouble than it was worth. This was another incentive to restrain military adventurism abroad. Henry V would beg to differ.

He was able to use his grip on the throne, and to start with an elite consensus that French assets were there for the taking, to win tax increases from Parliament which would not have flown to his father. As observed above, though, this was not an open chequebook. He would leave behind little money.

Foreign Policy

Foreign policy was France and that was about the end of it. Where other players were involved – for example, Sigismund, the Holy Roman Emperor, who spent months in England in 1416 – it was all about obtaining formal agreement that Henry was entitled to the throne of France once it had become vacant. His approach to Scotland was contingent on whether the Scots were aligning with his French foes.

On the face of it, Henry's record in France and hence the virtues of his foreign policy might speak for themselves and at volume in his acclamation. The Treaty of Troyes could be adduced to serve as proof of this. However, a series of counter-observations can be marshalled to suggest that Henry's foreign policy was less stellar.

He could have pressed home his advantage after Agincourt more effectively. There was no French army of any meaningful form in its aftermath. The road to Paris was there to be taken. Instead, mainly because he had stretched an insufficient number of men to their limit, he had to take time out. He was content to allow the Burgundy and Orléans aristocracies to engage in civil war. It was only when the former defeated the latter while exhausting itself that he was able to enter Paris and press terms.

Having returned to England to witness the coronation of his wife (and leave her behind pregnant), it was a mistake to dash back to France when he did. It placed him in unnecessary danger. He was motivated by venom after his brother Thomas (the Duke of Clarence) had managed to get himself killed in a needless raid in the Loire, which placed him in the path of an otherwise irrelevant Franco-Scottish set of soldiers. The siege of Meaux, which preoccupied Henry in the summer of 1422, was the sort of mopping-up operation that could and should have been entrusted to others. If he had to be in France at all (which is contestable), he would have been better off consolidating his authority in Paris, running the clock down and being in the right place at the right time for the death of Charles VI, who would instead outlast Henry by a matter of a few weeks.

The much more profound question to address is whether, if Henry had indeed headed towards Paris, avoided whatever malady robbed him of life, and been crowned King of France in late 1422, this would have actually served his own best interests from then on, or those of England.

There is a robust set of assertions to be made that it would not have worked out as he wanted. Charles VI had disinherited his dauphin (who would become Charles VII). He remained the legitimate candidate to be king, was at liberty and would have attracted protection from those who did not want to see France fall into the hands of a foreigner. The fears that he would have the personal failings of his father, dubbed 'Charles the Mad', were false; after his death, Charles VII would be known as 'Charles the Victorious'. Without the expired king's son either imprisoned by him or dead, Henry V was in for more conflict.

Even if those conditions had been met, factional politics in France would certainly have surfaced. Were the Burgundians to be satisfied by the modest rewards which they might have obtained if Henry V had also been Henry II of France, or would they have demanded immense amounts of land, which if offered would have somewhat undermined the purpose of becoming king in the first place? If Dauphin Charles had not been the catalyst for combat, then the Burgundians could have been.

There is a more fundamental dimension to consider. If we assume, and it is quite a leap of faith, that Henry had lived, placed himself on the French throne and not faced consequential resistance to his rule, how was the administration of England and France to operate? Human cloning was no closer in his age than in our own. How would he have divided his time between the two capitals? Where would his queen (a vital element in producing a plentiful supply of potential heirs) have been located? Who would have been his regent in France when Henry was in England (the Duke of Burgundy had his eye on that role for good reason), or his regent in England when Henry was in France (his favoured brother Thomas being deceased)? Would England and France have been one country or two? If he had produced multiple children, would the nations have been divided later? There is no evidence that these crucial factors had been subject to anything like rigorous analysis.

Norman Davies, in his incomparable account of British history, *The Isles* (published in 1999), put it well:

Henry V (1413–22)

He [Henry V] would have been leading both his own family and his English homeland into a high-risk lottery. In which case instead of bemoaning his untimely death, English patriots should rest content that he died when he did.

Succession

On that death, Henry left behind a 9-month-old son to succeed him. A regency scarred by a dispute between two of his brothers (John, Duke of Bedford, and Humphrey, Duke of Gloucester) followed. Everything unravelled in France with Joan of Arc emerging to allow Charles VII to remain as king.

It would, in fairness, have been even more desperate if Henry had died childless. Henry IV had left him with five siblings. Thomas predeceased him with no legitimate issue. John would not have any children at all. Humphrey only had a child outside wedlock. Philippa, Henry's sister, the Queen of Denmark, Sweden and Norway, expired childless. Only Blanche, another sister, who was married to Louis III, the Elector of the Palatine, produced a son, Rupert, in 1406 (he died in 1426 childless). Anarchy threatened the Lancastrian strain of the House of Plantagenet after Henry V died.

That he was a great (if sadistic) soldier is not to be denied. Yet Henry V is an overrated king. His much despised and partially deformed father, Henry IV, would measure better on the metrics of monarchy.

Henry VII (1485–1509)

UNDERRATED

When all the circumstances surrounding his reign are considered, there is a powerful argument that Henry VII was the most perceptive and professional monarch ever to sit on the throne of England. He has a reputation as a miser and certainly had none of the extravagance which would be associated with his heirs, but they were only in a position to engage in exhibitionism because they were secure in their status courtesy of the founding father of the Tudor dynasty. Henry VII may have had a style and personality that smacked more of Clement Attlee than Winston Churchill, but much like Attlee, in a comparatively short time he reconstituted the kingdom that he acquired in a fundamental fashion.

The Challenge

Henry VII faced three interconnected challenges which would set the scene for his entire tenure, but which also explain the remorseless determination with which he would pursue his personal agenda.

The first concerned the strength of his own blood claim to the throne. It was feeble. It is probably the least compelling of any of the figures whose actions as monarch are sketched in this volume. This was a serious liability for him when he attempted to become king, and it would mean that there was always the risk – indeed, more than a risk, for there were multiple actual and suppressed rebellions against him – that his right to the Crown would come under scrutiny and that active measures would have to be taken to maintain his authority. This was a reign based on extremely shaky foundations.

Both sides of his family brought complexities in making the case that he was the rightful monarch.

On his father's side, the thesis was threadbare. The alleged noble line came through Owen Tudor, Henry's grandfather, who had been a loyal but not especially senior lieutenant to Henry V. In what would have seemed a shocking attempt at acquiring upward mobility, Owen appears to have wed Catherine of Valois, the widow of his former monarchical master, in secret (it was certainly not a bond which would have been permitted if publicly floated). A consequence of this marriage (if we assume this was indeed what occurred) was the birth of Henry's father, Edmund Tudor. During a lull in the hostilities which consumed much of Henry VI's reign, Edmund was formally declared to be legitimate by Parliament in 1452 (an initiative which at a minimum demonstrates that his status was open to question) and was rendered the Earl of Richmond, a solid title of the nobility, to be sure, but not one of the very highest tier. In any case, the new earl became entangled in the poisonous politics of his era as the rifts between the Lancastrians and Yorkists became ever more intense, and he would die in a murky manner (murder is a strong candidate) three months before his only child, Henry, was born.

His mother had only modestly stronger credentials. She was undoubtedly descended from John of Gaunt, son of Edward III, by his third wife, Katherine Swynford. She had been his mistress for many years before he finally made the proverbial honest woman of her. At the time of their marriage, she had already borne four children, including John Beaufort, from whom Margaret of Beaufort, Henry's mother, would assert her royal standing. There was an obvious difficulty here, that of illegitimacy.

There appears to have been a consensus from the top that this had to be swept under the carpet. In 1397, Richard II legitimised the children (precisely on what basis it is not straightforward to divine) and this was reaffirmed with a twist by the man who usurped him as king, Henry IV, a decade later. Henry was himself descended from John of Gaunt but through his first wife (whom he understandably placed a higher premium on than the third one), so while the legitimacy was maintained, this clan was declared ineligible for the succession (thus diluting the legitimation). Whether Henry IV was in any position to do this is contentious, as Parliament had endorsed the family as legitimate and as a potential avenue to the throne. To some extent, this was mud that could stick to Henry Tudor.

From the moment of his birth in January 1457, Henry Tudor was in a potentially precarious position. With his father dead, he relied on his uncle, Jasper Tudor, as his protector. But the intricacies and intrigue around the monarchy made him a less than reliable guarantor of young Henry's security. He would flee when Edward IV managed to overthrow Henry VI in 1461. This left the young aspirant in the care of William Herbert, a staunch Yorkist, who became the Earl of Pembroke at Edward IV's behest. Mercifully for the juvenile Henry, he was not considered to be a credible contender for the Crown at this moment, and neither his life nor his liberty was in dire danger while he remained in remote Wales.

All that changed once more when the fabled Richard Neville, 'Warwick the Kingmaker', switched sides (again) and aligned with the Lancastrian cause and the attempt to restore Henry VI to power. He captured Herbert and had him executed. In the short term this was a boon to Henry Tudor, in that with Henry VI back in command (at least notionally), Henry's uncle, Jasper Tudor, could return to London and introduce his nephew to the court for the first time. This elevated situation did not last for long. Edward IV duly made his comeback and the Tudor family had to take hasty flight to Brittany.

This would result in a long exile with the periodic possibility that it would end in chains back to England. From 1471 to 1485, Henry Tudor would live on the continent, relying on the support of others for his freedom. This meant the continued favour of Frances II, Duke of Brittany, which was at the risk of withdrawal either because of his own calculations or because he was ill or distracted. Henry came very close to being deported in 1476 and might not have lasted long if he had been.

By a process of elimination, he became steadily more important in the question of the succession. The 'elimination' was that of his more esteemed relatives. By 1483, Henry VI was long dead as were his son Edward, Prince of Wales, and the descendants of Edmund Beaufort, 2nd Duke of Somerset, who might have had a more convincing bloodline than a child of Margaret Beaufort. On the Yorkist side, Edward IV was deceased and any prospect of a smooth succession through his offspring had been upended by Edward V and his brother Richard first being denounced as illegitimate by an Act of Parliament inspired by their uncle, Richard III, then disappearing. Richard's credentials were undercut by his actions. All of a sudden, Henry Tudor looked like a plausible alternative to Richard III and appeared to be the most likely Lancastrian contender should the chance arise. With his claim still less than stellar, however, Henry sought to shore it up by asserting that if crowned king he would wed Elizabeth of York (Edward IV's daughter and sister of Edward V and Prince Richard) and end the strife over the throne.

This had to be achieved in practice. This was the second challenge that Henry had to overcome. The fifteenth century was littered with aspiring monarchs landing somewhere in the British Isles, being hailed by their supporters and either having to withdraw or entering battle and being slaughtered.

This could so easily have been Henry's fate as well. It was more likely than not. In August 1485, he set off with a distinctly modest and motley collection of French and Scottish recruits as his army (how much they could have been trusted if the going had got tough is doubtful). He landed in Wales, where he hoped that his local roots might allow him to drum up more forces, although their quality if they responded to the call to arms was uncertain. Having reached at most 6,000 men (quite probably fewer), they marched in the direction of England, intending to meet Richard III in battle.

This was an encounter which the incumbent monarch had reason to feel confident about. He had a fearsome reputation as a warrior, had the larger of the two sets of troops, and had access to many fresh recruits inside Leicester and Nottingham if he needed them. Bosworth Field was also not ideal terrain for Henry and his troops to dominate. This was a contest which should have ended with Henry Tudor either dead or defeated and scrambling back to a coastline.

It did not. It would be harsh to describe Henry's victory at Bosworth Field as a fluke, but it was rather fortunate. A series of miscalculations, desertions (notably by the Stanley family) and a deliberate withholding of support in the field (Exhibit A: Henry Percy, the 4th Duke of Northumberland) were to prove Richard III's undoing. Even then, if he had managed to retreat and regroup, he might well have defeated Henry at the second time of asking. As it was, he found himself ejected from his horse in the midst of a skirmish that he could and should have avoided, and was killed immediately afterwards. It would be the last time that the throne would be determined by the sword and not succession.

Henry Tudor had become Henry VII, but that merely meant that the third and final challenge awaited him. How would he hold on to that which had fallen into his grasp? There would be scores of Yorkists who considered the events of Bosworth Field to be only a temporary setback. His blood claim to the throne remained extremely contestable. The nobility had become a force in the land on their own terms, in a manner that had echoes of more than 250 years earlier. The monarch would have to press hard to be seen as much more than first among equals. The Treasury was empty. Foreign powers had become accustomed to meddling in the affairs of England and then calling in their debts if their chosen upstart managed to obtain the throne. Henry was a king with barely a kingdom.

In order to confront this state of affairs, Henry would need to show something close to mastery on all five of the fronts that it has been asserted here are the appropriate measures for sound monarchy.

Professional Standing

Henry VII started to consolidate his authority by an atypical means, the prerogative of mercy. He acted as if his elevation to the throne had of itself drawn the unfortunate matters of the past few decades to a welcome close. By the standards of the time, he would have been within his rights to put Richard III's nephew and designated heir, the Earl of Lincoln, to the executioner's block there and then, but he did not do so. He allowed him to remain at comparatively unrestricted liberty. He made the Yorkist heiress, Margaret Plantagenet, the Countess of Salisbury in her own right. He sensed that he could not take the risk of allowing the Earl of Warwick, the 10-year-old son of Edward IV's brother, the Duke of Clarence, to wander around at will, as it would be too easy for Yorkist dissidents to co-opt him to their cause, so he was transported to the Tower of London but not treated very harshly. He was similarly benign to the Earl of Warwick's elder sister, Margaret, who would survive until 1541 when Henry VIII in one of his fits of enthusiasm for government by execution would deal with her. He had Parliament repeal the *Titulus Regius*, the means by which Richard III had Edward IV's offspring designated illegitimate, which could have inflated the standing of some of the possible rivals to him. Finally, with her illegitimacy cast off, he made good on his pre-battle pledge to marry Elizabeth of York, to whom he would prove an unusually devoted husband with not the slightest hint of infidelity.

In different conditions, these actions could have been seen as weakness, not resilience or a desire to bring to a conclusion a long, bloody and thoroughly disruptive age of score-settling. However, Henry stuck with it. The first serious rebellion of his reign took place when Lambert Simnel, a youth set up to impersonate the Earl of Warwick, who remained in the Tower of London, claimed to be the rightful monarch. Simnel was crowned in Dublin and arrived in London with the backing of an Irish force. The rebellion quashed, Henry responded by sending Simnel to work in his palace kitchens, overseeing the spit roast rather than being toasted on it, and pardoned the Irish nobles who had supported this improbable revolution. He then spent several years being irritated and inconvenienced by another fraud, Perkin Warbeck, who pretended to be Richard, younger brother of Edward V, who it was said had escaped the Tower and lived on the run. When Henry finally had Warbeck in his possession, it was his instinct to keep him under house arrest, until Warbeck's itch for continued meddling proved so intense that he had to be executed. At that point, and as the only figure to whom Yorkists might rally, in 1499 the Earl of Warwick also died. Perhaps Henry recognised, in the fragile lives of these various young characters, echoes of his own very uneasy existence from 1457 to 1485, but regardless, it is striking how reluctant he was to shed blood.

This was, nonetheless, an example of the iron fist in the velvet glove. Henry was dedicated to taking the Crown back to its former glories and that meant bringing much of the nobility to heel, even if it was unlikely that they would lose their heads on his orders. He used bonds and recognisances with gusto in order to demonstrate his authority and entrench loyalty to him. When lands became free due to vacant possession or childless death among great families, they would be appropriated to him. In the preceding somewhat lawless decades, certain nobles had formed the habit of living as if they were mini-kings in their own domain, with elaborate forms of livery or maintaining an excessive number of male servants as effectively a private mercenary army. Henry cracked down on this hard and was largely effective at obliging others to pay fidelity to him. There were exceptions to this rule (the Stanley family, for instance), but they did not push their luck.

This extension of personal control and with it the compounding of the professional standing of the king often required institutional innovation with which Henry was more than comfortable. In his time, the Star Chamber came into its own as the device for resolving disputes among the nobles, with the more unwieldy Privy Council relegated as a consequence. Henry alighted on a network of justices of the peace both to preserve order and to act as a form of intelligence agency for him. He expanded their number on an epic scale, so that there was one for every shire. Their appointment was reviewed annually and their remit checked so that they could not become little kings in themselves. That they were all obliged to operate unpaid suited Henry's other leading priorities.

Although he became a more isolated and withdrawn figure in his final years (markedly so after the deaths of, first, Prince Arthur in 1502, and then Queen Elizabeth in 1503), Henry had acquired the professional standing which allowed the machine that he had built to hum with a foot off the pedal. Few, if any, monarchs have won such a professional standing from such an unstable initial position.

Henry VII (1485–1509)

Public Opinion

As far as we can tell – and the sources at this time are far from forensic – public opinion was the weakest of the measurements for monarchical success in Henry VII's case. There is not much evidence that he was particularly popular, and his death does not seem to have been the source of much sorrow. On the other hand, he does not appear to have been actively unpopular, in that the many attempts at rebellion against him invariably ran out of steam and did not catch fire.

The blunt truth is that, at this time, if a king had effective hegemony over the bulk of the nobility, then wider public opinion was a very secondary consideration. One area which could inspire discontent was the Church, but Henry's appointments were solidly meritocratic, and he had no interest in being the cause of any controversy in his realm. He lavished attention on Westminster Abbey and paid for the construction of King's College Chapel, Cambridge. Church sentiment would have been with him.

The one area where Henry took some chances with public opinion was on taxation. Whereas the habit of previous monarchs had been to wage (often pricey) wars first and think about how these enterprises might be paid for afterwards (or to underfund them in the first instance), Henry's outlook was entirely the opposite. If there was the slightest prospect of conflict expenditure on the horizon (and France and Scotland always meant this might flare up), then he would rather have the money in the bank in advance, and if in the end little or no fighting materialised, then he was not in much of a rush to send coinage back to those who had contributed it. As will be outlined later, this was not so much about wild personal profligacy (he was not that type) as about his preference for a rainy-day fund.

This was all very well, but those taxed can be excused their disagreement with losing the money. Henry was not oblivious to public opinion beyond the ranks of the highest estates, and he had a sense of how much he could demand before the resulting unpopularity brought more cost than benefit. As Jean-Baptist Colbert, Louis XIV's finance minister, memorably remarked much later: 'The art of taxation consists in so plucking the goose as to obtain the largest amount of feathers with the smallest amount of hissing.'[4] Henry VII did not always strike that balance, but he was not far off it.

Financial Competence

As implicit above, whereas previous monarchs had often sought military glory regardless of the cost, Henry VII would rather have been an accountant than a knight in shining armour. His long (and often comparatively impoverished) time in exile had left him little opportunity to acquire prior experience in fiscal management or estate economics, but he accumulated it rapidly once king. What others might have regarded as a mundane or tedious part of the position, Henry threw himself into.

Record keeping and elementary financial planning in the decades before the first Tudor monarchy had more or less collapsed. Henry reversed that situation. Not only did he take an extraordinary interest in the numbers himself, he also sought out talented associates and retained their service. Baron Dynham and the Earl of Surrey spent much of his reign as the Lord High Treasurers. To extract bounty from the nobility, Henry called in Archbishop John Morton as his chancellor (men of God frequently doubled up as men of mammon in this era). The masses did not need a man of the cloth to tax them, so those of a more lowly birth, but manifest abilities, were recruited for that purpose. Richard Empson and Edmund

---

4   *Oxford Essential Quotations* (6th edition), edited by Susan Ratcliffe (2018).

Henry VII (1485–1509)

Dudley served Henry well as his principal tax collectors for much of his tenure. Their reward was arrest and execution at the hands of Henry VIII in a ploy of pure populism. If there were a sofa, then Henry VII's men would find some lost coins in it. Money mattered to this monarch as a source of political security as well as offering him crucial financial flexibility in his many dealings.

Henry understood that trade was central to national wealth, while warfare was often a drain upon it. He became the leading player in the alum trade (a highly sought-after dye for wool), even though no alum could be found in England itself but only in a small plot of modern Italy controlled by the papacy. This did not prevent Henry from becoming the indispensable middleman in the alum arrangement. To harden his negotiating hand, he managed to start a squabble with the Burgundian Netherlands on the pretext of protesting the machinations of Margaret of Burgundy, sister of Edward IV, who had never recognised his right to succeed her brother and among other provocations allied herself with Perkin Warbeck, vouching for his authenticity as the lost Prince Richard. Henry forced the Flemish merchants out of England, prompted the Merchant Adventurers with whom he was closely linked to relocate from Antwerp to Calais, and maintained the commercial pressure until he obtained a reward in the form of the *Magnus Intercursus* of 1496, which confirmed his dominance of the alum industry. Looking to far further shores, he backed the Cabot brothers in their expeditions to Newfoundland, an imaginative wager that not only made a tidy profit but gave England its opening to the Americas.

Financial intelligence would also be a substantial element in Henry's activist personal foreign policy.

Foreign Policy

In so far as England had a foreign policy in the sixty or so years before Henry came to throne, it was about France. Or, put differently, it was about the quest to reclaim lands in what is contemporary France that had been obtained under Henry V but subsequently lost or, as a Plan B, to do what was required to prevent any other power assuming full control of French territory at England's expense. The distractions involved with civil insurrection and the disputes between Lancastrians and Yorkists had undermined whatever might have been achieved within France, although a shrewd monarch, as Henry VII plainly was, would have recognised that the empire of Henry V was never coming back.

Henry was content to play politics in France but not burn his stockpile of cash in the enterprise. He approached this with a cool pragmatic indifference to anything akin to principle. In 1489, he signed the Treaty of Redon in which he was effectively paid to defend Brittany from France. He changed tack in 1492 with the Peace of Étaples, a bargain with Charles VIII of France in which, among its clauses, Henry agreed to accept Charles's claim to be the ruler of the duchy of Brittany in exchange for Paris dropping its support for Perkin Warbeck's idiosyncratic bid to be deemed King of England. The fine print of this accord also assisted Henry's economic interests.

The English king always remained wary of his French counterparts. Appeasement through marriage offers was always an option (his daughter Mary would be briefly Queen of France before her new husband died). Offence being the best form of defence, Henry took steps to subsidise shipbuilding and reached into his pockets to fund the first dry dock seen in Europe, at Portsmouth in 1495. As part of his encirclement ethos on France, he also formed an alliance with Maximilian I, the Holy Roman Emperor, and was on cordial terms with Popes Innocent VII and Julius II. As in so many other aspects of his reign, Henry did not have an especially strong hand to play, but he played it well. Sensing the chance to undermine the 'Auld Alliance' between France and Scotland, Henry pressed for the Treaty of Perpetual Peace in 1502, to end, or at a minimum reduce, conflict with Scotland.

Where he turned out to be a visionary was in seeing the potential of Spain. That country had only just achieved a form of unity after divisions which ran deeper than those of England. It had yet to become massively enriched by gold and silver from the New World, as these were early days in its presence in central and south America. Despite this, Henry sought out Spain as a partner and settled as early as 1489 on the Treaty of Medina del Campo, best remembered because it was the means by which Catherine of Aragon would enter the English royal household (it also reduced trade tariffs).

Succession

The blighted Catherine of Aragon would eventually become part of a succession crisis for Henry VIII and Tudor England. This was not self-evident at the time of Henry VII's death. He had done his duty (as, obviously, had his queen, Elizabeth) in terms of oiling the wheels of an effortless handover.

The couple had six children, although only three of them would live to be full adults. Arthur had been the eldest son and the one promised at a young age to be the husband of Catherine of Aragon. She had arrived on English shores in 1501 for their marriage. In what was perhaps the biggest mishap of Henry's tenure, the Prince of Wales died (it is thought of consumption) in 1502, taking a wrecking ball to his diplomatic strategy.

What to do next with Catherine of Aragon suddenly became an unsettled matter of high policy. One possibility momentarily considered when Henry became a widower a year later was that he himself might take her as a bride. It was eventually decided that although he was younger than her, Prince Henry should marry his former sister-in-law, and the necessary papal dispensation to make this acceptable was obtained.

The loss of Arthur did not mean that the succession would be menaced. Henry was a strong young man. He would take the throne in 1509 with minimal argument. The path had been laid for him. In optimal circumstances, it would have been preferable for there to have been another son as well, but the absence of such a sibling was not a tragedy. There were two daughters who would be good prizes on the matrimonial market. Margaret, the older of the two, would be the bride of James IV, a selection which a century later would unite the thrones of England and would bear an heir, James V. Mary would be the third wife of Louis XII of France (although he died less than three months after she was crowned), and soon after she returned to England, she would be wed to the Duke of Suffolk. There was little reason in 1509 to fear that the Tudors did not have enough numbers to endure. It was not of Henry's making that there would be a succession issue later on. He did not bequeath one.

While historians have long lauded Henry VII's skill as king, he has not seized the wider imagination. To that extent he truly is an astonishingly underrated figure. When he died, he was seen as 'the richest prince in Christendom'. As James Gairdner put it in the famed 1910–11 edition of the *Encyclopædia Britannica*: 'He not only terminated a disastrous civil war and brought under control the spirit of ancient feudalism, but with a clear survey of foreign powers he gave England an almost uninterrupted peace while he developed her commerce.' The greatest of English kings was actually a Welshman.

Henry VIII (1509–47)

OVERRATED

If charisma were considered to be the currency of the realm when it comes to monarchical quality, then there would not be much of a contest. Henry VIII would be on any short list and a plausible victor. If the test is broadened out beyond charisma to being captivating, then his position would be even stronger. It is not merely his collection of six wives which should secure attention, although perhaps strangely this Hollywood element to his personal story is a large element in his standing. It is the extent to which he sought to remodel his kingdom in his own image and very much in his personal interests.

A part of the portrait of this larger-than-life figure (in more ways than one) was essentially propaganda. All the Tudors, perhaps quietly aware of the tenuous nature of their initial claim to the throne, were inclined towards promoting their virtues, but while this was a relatively modest feature of life in the reign of Henry VII, it was much more pronounced under his second son (as it would be in turn with Henry VIII's second daughter). The notion of 'Good King Henry', who might occasionally be led astray by advisers who conspired against the interests of the common people behind his back, was a theme constantly repeated. It would continue until the very last days of his thirty-eight-year reign.

The positive spin (to adopt modern parlance) has lasted into the twenty-first century. Its features are now familiar. The new king was young (just 17 at the hour of his succession). He was also strikingly tall, especially when compared with his contemporaries. Height can be a huge advantage in leadership, hammering home the notion of predestined superiority. Even in the 1940s and 1950s, Charles de Gaulle's stature (he was around 6ft 6in at full stretch, about a full foot taller than his typical fellow countryman) compounded the notion that he was the natural saviour of France. The young Henry was also (apparently) handsome in an age when court portrait images began to have a wider circulation than they had done previously and became an instrument of prestige. He was a distinguished athlete, not least at jousting and associated armoured sports, at a moment when the whole concept of chivalry was undertaking something of a revival across vast swathes of Europe.

He also fitted the broader sense of what we would now call a Renaissance prince (it is less obvious that observers of monarchs then would have related to such terminology). He was an intellectual. He spoke several languages. He was a patron of the arts and of painters, notably Holbein. He was an author and (possibly) a composer himself. He was certainly eloquent about music. He was on good terms with Erasmus, which raised estimates of his own status as a part-time philosopher. In the early years of his tenure, he must have seemed like a breath of fresh air compared with his austere father.

Charisma is not, though, the lode star of leadership. If it is the icing on a cake made of more relevant material, then it is indeed a considerable virtue. If it is, or becomes, a substitute for substance, then it is a vice in the making. The reign of Henry VIII was one of enormous turmoil for his subjects as well as those who served at his pleasure in positions of authority. Although this is partly because this was an era of upheaval across Europe, a disproportionately large amount was due to the king himself. This manifested itself in personal authoritarianism, which frequently crossed the line into tyranny, a deep disinterest in affairs of state that did not directly impact on him, and an extraordinary effect on the religious life of England, more dramatic in many respects than in other nations at that time.

It would not be much of an exaggeration to describe Henry VIII as the combination of Louis XIV of France and Joseph Stalin of the Soviet Union. Henry as much as the future French king believed and lived by the notion that 'L'état c'est moi'. The subtle checks and balance in the unwritten, unstated but not unappreciated constitutional settlement that had been in place since the Magna Carta of 1215 would be challenged on a continuous basis. Authority was to be centralised in the person of the king with Parliament returned to the role of rubber stamp, the Church, as will be outlined, was castrated as an independent force, and Wales more thoroughly (through the Laws of Wales Act, 1535) and in a more limited fashion Ireland (following a royal declaration of 1542) were to be bound closer. The concept of the royal prerogative was expanded exponentially with not merely the Privy Council but also the Star Chamber largely rendered, to borrow from Walter Bagehot's later words, a 'dignified' rather than an 'efficient' element of the constitutional order. There was never any chance that the king would be obliged to change course because of opposition from the nobility. It was rather more probable that nobles individually and collectively would be forced to change course at the behest of the king.

A mighty contributory cornerstone to all this was simple fear. Henry VII had been very cautious in his approach to enemies or prospective opponents, reaching for the executioner's axe as a last resort. He had more subtle instruments to hand to translate his will into the law of the land. His son had no such inhibitions.

Those who crossed him were unlikely to be pardoned or imprisoned softly. A visit to the Tower of London was neither a season ticket nor one where a return trip would be forthcoming. To a degree which stood out from others who sat on the throne before or after, the risk of execution would have to be accepted as part of the conditions of service. That was true whether one was the queen consort (as two would discover), the most loyal of servants (Thomas Cromwell), a close friend (Sir Thomas More), an eminent clergyman (Bishop Fisher of Rochester) or those of a humbler rank who had participated in the Pilgrimage of Grace and been explicitly offered clemency (including Robert Aske and scores of others who were tracked down, arrested and then executed).

Many of those who met their end under the king's constitution were not even allowed a token aspect of due process. Trials would be bypassed in favour of a simple Bill of Attainment. Although nothing took place which could come anywhere close to the sadistic Soviet purges, the lack of legal process makes the comparison with Stalin plausible. No other English monarch, not even those imbued with the Divine Right of Kings, has been so willing to dispose of their subjects.

Yet although Henry clearly considered that he embodied the constitution, he was disinterested to the point of dereliction when it came to anything resembling the details of public administration. He was focused on marriages (too many) and money (too little) and all else was deemed to be beneath him. In the earliest part of his reign, when tournaments at home and adventures abroad filled his time, he delegated extensively to Archbishop Warham (his Lord Chancellor), Bishop Foxe and the Earl of Surrey. It fell to them to somehow locate the resources which allowed the king to follow his fancies.

When this trio had peaked in influence, it would be Thomas Wolsey who supplanted all of them. A man of undoubted ability but also insatiable ambition and Olympic avarice, the later

Henry VIII (1509–47)

Cardinal Wolsey would take so much of the tedium of paperwork and planning out of the king's hands that he was to all intents and purposes the acting monarch on a day-to-day basis. Exactly what Henry would have done if his various schemes to see Wolsey elevated to the papacy had come to fruition is a mystery. When his downfall came, as invariably would be true for even the most senior counsellors, he too would probably have finished his life in the Tower of London had he not wisely died beforehand.

After him came Thomas Cromwell. He followed the familiar pattern of ingratiation into Henry's confidence, spectacular hard work and not inconsiderable flair to remodel government to suit the monarch's needs, personal enrichment, envy attracted from factions within the highest ranks of the nobility and a sudden end. After 1540, when Cromwell lost his head, it was the turn of Thomas Cranmer to assume the reins of chief minister and be there with his leader until his deathbed at the end (only for the monarch's daughter to send him to the flames a few years after).

Archbishop Cranmer is also a critical player in what was the most massive convulsion of them all, the fundamental reorganisation of faith in order to satisfy Henry VIII's dynastic requirements. Much of Europe was in a state of flux over religion after Martin Luther had launched his attack on the papacy, which then snowballed into a full-scale assault on the Roman Catholic Church itself. A side effect of this would be an eruption of cults and self-appointed prophets or aspiring messiahs. The opening response of Henry VIII to all this had been to support old orthodoxy unflinchingly. His *Defence of the Seven Sacraments* published in 1521 was dedicated to Leo X and it is doubtful whether that Pope disagreed with a single word of it. Henry's devotion to the see of Rome would be rewarded by the award of the title *Fidei Defensor* in 1524, which two decades later the king would have Parliament embody in law for his successors, even though he himself had by then been excommunicated.

What Henry had once insisted was the Word of God would count for little when the Bishop of Rome would not come up with a formula which would allow him to ease Catherine of Aragon out as his queen, install Anne Boleyn and engage in a belated (in the end, ineffective) dash for a son to be his heir and preserve the Tudor lineage, which was in danger of being extinguished after two men. Protestantism of several forms was being adopted across much of northern Europe, but only in England did the monarch in effect appoint himself Pope through the concept of the creation of a Supreme Governor of the Church of England. In so far as there was a theological rationale that came with this switch, it was the work of Cranmer who, in fairness to him, did try to seek a semblance of intellectual validity by bolting on those aspects of continental Protestantism that Henry would take. Otherwise, it was not only a matter of 'L'état c'est moi' but also 'Le dieu c'est moi'.

The sheer force of this change in the lives of ordinary people as well as nobles of conscience is hard to overstate. Religion was fundamental to life. It was the purpose of life for millions of individuals. It had been hard-wired into social understanding. The overthrow of the Pope in England was not just a shuffling of the ecclesiastical pack but an enormous jolt to daily existence. Henry had adopted what was functionally a state religion because it suited him. In the 1530s, he made moves to accommodate what he had done. By the 1540s, with a son and heir now on the scene, he had second thoughts and reverted to a more conservative direction. Having meted out his version of justice to those who had clung to the old faith and taken part in the Pilgrimage of Grace, he became more concerned about the activities of religious radicals such as the Lollards and the various advocates of an imminent end to the world and a final alignment with the Almighty, which suddenly acquired popular acclamation during the extraordinary summer of 1540 when months of heat were seen as a sign of Apocalypse.

Henry VIII (1509–47)

Irrespective of where one stands on whether Henry VIII is underrated or overrated as a monarch (and that will be addressed very shortly), that he was the most disruptive of kings must be certain. Henry VIII also ranks badly on the metrics for measuring monarchy.

Professional Standing

In a sense because he had such a transformative impact on what had previously been regarded as 'the rules of the game', professional standing mattered less for Henry VIII than his predecessors. This was precisely the problem with how he chose to organise his affairs. The implicit checks and balances of times past were largely dispensed with. What replaced them was an orgy of obsequiousness at the top as different noble families sought to win his favour, often through their daughters as his wives.

The politics of patronage became pre-eminent. There was a stark divide between those to whom Henry had handed unprecedented autonomy to act in his name (often acquiring incredible wealth as part of the package), such as Thomas Wolsey and Thomas Cromwell, and those who deemed that they were born to the great families of England, who had always expected a degree of respect as a result. This might be labelled 'creative tension' by some, but it was more a matter of fear and favour than anything else. After Henry's death there was an undeclared agreement among those for whom his professional standing should have counted for more that this was not an experiment to be repeated. This would have been true even if Edward VI had been older and healthier when he became king. Henry had taken England to an uncomfortable extreme not seen for three centuries or more, if ever.

Public Opinion

In so far as it can be assessed — and that is an awkward exercise — the traditional narrative of the young Henry VIII being largely cheered by his subjects, mostly from a very considerable distance, is probably accurate and may have held until religious divisions and economic distress hit home. It is certainly what the new king appears to have wanted (unlike his father, who preferred to be respected rather than either fêted or feared). As Lady Antonia Fraser observed of the Henry VIII phenomenon: 'Unlike Henry VII, the new King showed himself to the people everywhere, for he knew that showmanship was a most necessary branch of statesmanship.'[5]

If so, then rock star royalty has rather deeper roots than might otherwise be envisaged. As time went on, nevertheless, the monarch spent much more time at court and less as a celebrity with a crown. The 1520s and 1530s were not an easy period in which to be a peasant, with several bad harvests. Whether these were noticed at a court dominated by 'the King's Great Matter' (his inability to obtain the divorce that he so desperately desired) is a subject for conjecture. It seems probable that after almost twenty years, the stardust which was attached to the youthful King had lost its sheen. Economic dislocation in rural England was apparent as nobles tightened the screw on smallholders.

The most visible sign of mass protest was undoubtedly the Pilgrimage of Grace of 1536, which arose in the north of England. This has been portrayed in some quarters as the biggest threat to his rule that Henry ever faced as king, but that has the smack of overstatement to it. As an event it was closer in aspiration and spirit to the Jarrow Crusade of exactly four centuries later than the storming of the Bastille or the seizure of the Winter Palace. The tone was one of sorrow, not anger, with most of those at

---

5 *The Lives of the Kings and Queens of England*, edited by Antonia Fraser, p. 177.

the helm of the movement convinced that if they could only set out their concerns in front of royal authority, then they would receive a positive response to their grievances. As noted previously, if that is what they had assumed, then they were destined for severe disappointment. The warm words served up at the height of the insurrection (if that is even the appropriate term for an exceptionally peaceful demonstration) were worth nothing at all as an increasingly paranoid king convinced himself that he could smell treason and sanctioned fierce retribution against the 'rebels'. It is hard to conceive that this would not have drained any remaining popular support for the king.

Financial Competence

If Henry VII had been an accountant who missed his vocation, Henry VIII was the polar opposite. He would not have had the slightest idea of what a ledger contained or any sense of fiscal discipline. In so far as this was resolved at all towards the final years of his tenure, it was through the dual effect of high inflation and a campaign of cultural vandalism towards the monasteries that shocked Europe. Tudor England under his command would have had to call in the IMF if it had been established.

It had all started very differently. Henry had inherited the sum of £1,200,000 from his father (or about £400 million in contemporary valuation) and like some crazed lottery winner went about blowing it in an astounding fashion. A large percentage of it went on private extravagance. As will become evident soon, a foreign policy which took little account of the cost of warfare would also be the source of financial forfeiture. None of his various chief ministers could restrain his instincts.

The pattern was set at the outset. Henry had to have the most impressive court in Europe. His early years were a torrent of tournaments and other forms of very lavish entertainment.

As Catherine of Aragon admitted in an oft-cited letter to her father (who was hardly a pauper himself): 'our time is spent in continuous festival'. If anything, matters became even more reckless financially when the new king found himself confronted with rival monarchs of a similar age or younger in the form of Francis I of France and Charles V of Spain. The staggering expenditure which took place in the encounter between Henry and Francis at the Field of the Cloth of Gold in 1520 is legendary.

This financial anarchism soon took its toll. Within five years of succeeding his father, the family coffers had been severely depleted. Various means were sought of bringing in more revenue, be that through asset sales, the solicitation of 'gifts' or more intense taxation of the nobles and peasants. It did not help that what money might be out there seemed to end up ensnared by Cardinal Wolsey. It was as much the sense that he had failed to deliver on the monetary needs of the king and closest circle as the endless delays in advancing his divorce that led to Wolsey's departure from office.

His death allowed the monarch some short-term relief by means of confiscation. Wolsey had assembled an amazing property portfolio which was the envy of virtually everyone in England, including its ruler. With the cardinal now in his grave, the chance for plunder (or, as the king would have seen it, restitution) suddenly existed. The trouble was that when he got his hands on the likes of a Hampton Court Palace or a Cardinal's College, Oxford (soon renamed Christ Church), Henry much preferred to enhance and expand it, meaning more expenditure, rather than sell it to others.

It was Thomas Cromwell who by accident or design alighted on a solution. It combined a religious reform which would move the Church of England more firmly in a Protestant direction (which the chief minister was all for) with hugely enhanced fiscal freedom for the monarch (Henry VIII's requirement). It would involve what was branded as the dissolution of the monasteries but turned out to be more akin to their desecration. It triggered a vast redistribution of wealth to the king's private finances. At least a fifth, potentially a quarter, of England's landed wealth would be involuntarily transferred.

This particular ball started rolling with the Suppression of Religious Houses Act of 1535. That was a mere legal prelude to the raid which was to follow. It started in earnest in 1536 and the assets seized were quickly bringing in the better part of £100,000 a year to coffers which had previously been empty. What might have originally been thought of as a swift surgical strike and not a calculated campaign was elevated into a policy crusade with a second wave of dissolution launched in 1539. An aspect of the ethos of a Cultural Revolution then kicked in as the real zealots went after the monks as well as their money and widened the assault to include the widespread destruction of shrines to the saints, a blitz that brought in comparatively little cash (although everything of value was monetised) but added the smack of theological triumphalism for those determined to eradicate the old religion. In less than a decade, centuries of history as well as the treasure that lurked within the monasteries had been eradicated. It was a high price to pay for restoring the financial stability of the monarchy.

Lamentably, it did not even provide for fiscal rectitude. Like an inebriated sailor (he is recalled as a founder of the Royal Navy), if Henry VIII had money, then he would spend it, not save it. The jackpot that the dissolution of the monasteries provided would subsidise more grand projects. These included the recasting of York Place, one of Cardinal Wolsey's former estates, into Whitehall Palace (at more than 24 acres arguably the largest such building in the western world). This was followed by St James's Palace in central London and the surreal palace of Nonsuch located out in Surrey. Anne Boleyn and Catherine Howard may both have ended up without their heads but not before they had encouraged the king to lose his when it came to disposing of his monastic windfall at massive speed.

So, even allowing for appropriated loot, drastic further monetary measures had to be settled on. The most obvious of these was the debasing of the coinage, which had started in the 1530s but now intensified. The external value of English money slumped compared with its foreign competitors. The secondary effect of this was inflation on a scale that knocked the English economy sideways. A man who had inherited a treasure trove from his father would bequeath nothing of the kind to his son.

Foreign Policy

Henry's crippling financial difficulties were in part the consequence of the foreign policy of his first decade or so on the throne and came severely to restrict his overseas options in his last decade.

Henry VII had been a demon diplomat. Henry VIII wanted far more prominent recognition than that. He had initially contemplated an alliance with Louis XII of France (whom he liked) but instead signed up with the Holy League forged by the Pope that included Spain and Venice against France. As part of this arrangement, Henry himself led an expedition across the Channel and into French territory. If it was an effort to emulate the Hundred Years' War, then it did not take him very far (but was costly). While he was out of the country, the Earl of Surrey actually prevailed in a real battle against the Scots at Flodden in 1513 which ended up with James IV deceased and Queen Margaret acting as a regent. Henry then flipped again and settled on a peace treaty with France that did not bring in any money.

This pattern of inconsistency in his approach towards other European powers and financial loss was to be repeated. The Treaty of London signed in 1518 was supposed to see England, France and

Spain put aside their differences and unite to meet a renewed surge of the Ottoman Empire in Europe, but the harmony did not hold for long (although it was a catalyst for the Field of the Cloth of Gold) and Spain would rout France at the Battle of Pavia in 1525 with Francis humiliatingly taken as a prisoner.

Henry sought to cut his losses by throwing his hat in the ring to become the Holy Roman Emperor, but the electors had no intention of looking beyond the Habsburg family, so Charles V plucked the prize. That left Spain the supreme authority across the continent, which made it even more improbable that the Pope (completely the puppet of the Spanish king by this stage) would be of assistance as Henry sought to be rid of Catherine of Aragon, the aunt of Charles V. Foreign policy was at a stalemate.

With domestic affairs now pressing (his multiple marriages and the reconstitution of a religion) and with few resources at hand to entertain more military adventures, England entered a period of not so splendid isolation. It had become a somewhat irrelevant diplomatic actor. The sole success was again in Scotland (and with Henry nowhere close to the action) where the Battle of Solway Moss in 1542 ended with the demise of James V, leaving his tiny infant daughter Mary as his heir. Henry then responded by pressing for her to marry Prince Edward. The Scottish Parliament vetoed this notion.

Succession

That Henry was thinking about whom the young Edward might wed was not unreasonable. The birth of his (always less than entirely healthy) son had not ended the succession crisis. It was probable that the ailing and enormously overweight king would die before his son reached the age of maturity.

Some effort was made to smooth the path that might lie ahead. Assisted by his final wife, Catherine Parr, reconciliation across

Henry's varied families was attempted. Mary and Elizabeth came back to court and were treated as princesses, not the illegitimate output of marriages disavowed later.

A Council of Regency was planned for the event of Henry's death to choose and supervise a person who would take responsibility for Edward before he could assume the throne in full (which he never did), with Henry averting what would have been micromanagement of that appointment. This was just as well as the boy king's uncle, the Duke of Somerset, ignored all this and seized power himself.

If Edward died childless, the king's will declared, the succession would move to Mary, and if she were not to produce an heir, the chain of command extended to Elizabeth. The descendants of Margaret, Queen of Scotland (which meant Mary, Queen of Scots), were cut out and those of her younger sister Mary were promoted instead. This would set the scene for the botched attempt to elevate Lady Jane Grey a few years later, while the exclusion of the Scottish section of the family would not transpire. In life, Henry could strive to rewrite the rules to suit himself. In death, others would often frustrate him.

This was hardly a succession scheme that seemed certain to stand the test of time. It did not. In this as in all the other measures of monarchy, Henry may have been larger than life but small in stature. He may be among the most famous of kings but far from a great one. Infamous would be more apt. The term 'overrated' errs on the side of the charitable. Historians disagree about him, but for this author, G.R. Elton hit the nail on the head in his 1953 analysis, dubbing him an 'ego-centric monstrosity'.[6]

---

6   G.R. Elton, *The Tudor Revolution in Government* (1953).

Elizabeth I (1558–1603)

OVERRATED

To describe Elizabeth I as 'overrated' might strike many observers as close to shocking. She is one of the leading figures of English history. She was clearly highly intelligent, charming and cunning. She had to navigate her way through some extremely challenging waters well before her ultimate ascent to the throne. At her birth, she was an intense disappointment to her father, Henry VIII, who clearly wanted a son and not a second daughter. At the age of 2, she lost her mother, Anne Boleyn, to an executioner after a trial in which at best sensationalist and at worst utterly fabricated charges of adultery and incest were aired. She was subsequently rendered illegitimate and, even if she had not been, appeared to have become a marginal figure with a brother and a sister ahead of her in the line of succession (were she to be returned to it, which as late as the early 1540s did not seem likely). When brought back to court in the last years of Henry VIII, it was on a potentially probationary basis.

The situation did not improve much after her father died, although at least his will reinforced her restored standing. She initially lived with her stepmother, Catherine Parr, who, having buried a trio of husbands already, had taken up with a fourth, Sir Thomas Seymour, with Henry VIII barely cold. He made totally inappropriate moves towards the young Elizabeth, and when his wife died in childbirth, he appeared tempted by the idea of making the princess his next bride, despite a sizeable gap in age.

There is not much evidence of enthusiasm for this on her part, but the issue became moot because Sir Thomas became embroiled in a plot to disrupt or depose the Duke of Somerset, Lord Protector to Edward VI, and was arrested and executed. Not long after, Somerset himself suffered a revolt against his rule and would lose his own head after his downfall. The next guardian of Edward VI, the Duke of Northumberland, clearly considered Elizabeth a potential pawn in his game of dynastic chess, one who could be obliged to wed in a fashion that suited his interests. She showed an independence of spirit, even then, which convinced him not to oblige the dying young king to skip over Mary Tudor for Elizabeth in his will, but to bypass both sisters for Lady Jane Grey. In retrospect, this was a lucky escape.

Elizabeth was now the presumed heir to Queen Mary were she to die childless. This was not a total blessing. As she did not share her half-sister's fervour for restoring the Roman Catholic religion, she was a walking potential figurehead for those who wanted to stick with the Protestant reformation. There were several plots against Mary, and some came close to implicating Princess Elizabeth as being aware of their existence, even if she was not an active participant in or a supporter of them. Mary was deeply wary of her. Her husband, Philip II of Spain, strictly speaking titled the King of England from 1554, as no concept of a prince consort for a queen by blood had been settled on, was more pragmatic, but the Spanish ambassador warned Mary that she would never be secure on the throne and in her theological ambitions while Elizabeth remained alive. The risk of death existed.

In the end, despite hostile interrogation and the possibility that she might be sent to the Tower of London (possibly for the shock effect to deter her from future intrigue), Elizabeth was released but sent to Woodstock under terms that were very close to house arrest. She would only be safe if Mary either produced a healthy child and successor or died before those urging her to crack down harder on her sister or somehow conjure up an alternative successor loyal to the papacy had their hour. It would prove to be the second of these scenarios when, after a phantom pregnancy, Mary died in 1558.

At a minimum, therefore, there is much to be admired in Elizabeth as a human being. She was a more interesting figure than Henry VII, less cruel than Henry VIII, less fanatical than either Edward VI or Mary. She deserves a place in the top half of monarchs of these islands. What is contestable, far more contestable, is whether the assumption of many that she should be at the top table is valid. She has benefited from a reputation with more than a hint of hyperbole and of outright myth to it. This can be demonstrated in three key respects: the notion of the 'Virgin Queen' as a virtue; the idea that her religious settlement framed in 1559 was a work of inspiration which settled the bitter disputes over the Church that had raged before her; and adulation for her 'victory' over the Armada.

The first of these is in many respects the most important. Elizabeth either refused point-blank to marry (and from there on have the opportunity to produce an heir) or was open to the notion but waited so long to make her choice that the moment had passed in terms of the chances of a child. For a long period, this has been seen by some as political astuteness of an exceptional form. If she had married, the thesis goes, then her own authority would have been diminished. Added to which, the notion runs further, there was simply no candidate to be her husband who would have been acceptable to all the constituencies at court and in the country at large whose view counted. Having determined (whether at the outset of her reign or at a later date) that she would not be wed, she was also wise not to nominate or even indicate the name of her successor as this would have made that figure the same focus for unwanted political scheming that she had been under Mary, and/or might have made the queen herself a 'lame duck' without the status needed to govern.

All the above is, to put it politely, very close to poppycock. Elizabeth's refusal to marry (and constant prevarication over the subject on the numerous times that the Privy Council and Parliament urged her, even publicly, to do so), the absence of a child heir, and her reticence to acknowledge the branch of her family that came through either Henry VIII's eldest sister (Margaret) or his younger one (Mary) or, in the abstract, some other set of relatives (unlikely but possible), meant that not only her reign but her country was convulsed by a continued constitutional crisis, one death from a catastrophe.

This deeply perturbed her senior courtiers, even if she would hear little or nothing of the discussion. Their fears were apparent and amplified as early as the fourth year of Elizabeth's reign. She had contracted smallpox and at one stage looked as if she might be swept away by it. If she died, who would come next? In pure blood terms, the primary contender was Mary, Queen of Scots, but the prospect of such an unstable figure, politically indebted to France and a robust Roman Catholic to boot, filled the London Establishment with horror. The alternative, via Mary's second marriage to the Duke of Suffolk, was her granddaughter Lady Catherine Grey, the sister of Lady Jane Grey.

The dilemma here is that while Lady Catherine was in one respect an excellent contender (she would satisfy the terms of Henry VIII's will and she also had two young, male, children), she was at the time a resident of the Tower of London, having secretly and without acquiring the permission of the queen, as required, married Edward Seymour, 1st Earl of Hertford, the son of the former Lord Protector, the Duke of Somerset, an act which so infuriated Elizabeth (who was not short of a temper) that she had them imprisoned and declared their wedlock, and by extension their offspring, to be illegitimate. There seemed little chance of a smooth succession unless (a) Lady Catherine and family were let out and (b) their marriage was considered legal once again. Elizabeth, although very ill, would not relent.

High society was in a tailspin. Increasingly strange proposals were floated out of panic. One was that if Elizabeth expired, England might become, in just the short term, it was hoped, a kind of aristocratic republic where Parliament would choose the monarch. Elizabeth's recovery ended that scare. There would be many other points of anguish, nonetheless, with an intensity which quickened after 1568 as Mary, Queen of Scots, was set on English soil, having been driven to abdicate, fleeing Scotland and leaving her baby son in the control of nobles, and so a rallying point for Roman Catholics. What would happen after Elizabeth I died became the elephant in the room, the enormous 'what if?' for English political life for almost the entire second half of the sixteenth century. Elizabeth must have known this but did nothing about it. She was not compelled to marry but could and should have been more forthcoming about the succession if she stayed single. Her silence was destabilising.

Once upon a time, it was widely believed that the Elizabethan religious settlement of 1559, allied with the Prayer Book issued in the same year and the Thirty-Nine Articles of 1563, represented a compromise that was at a level close to genius, and which satisfied the overwhelming bulk of the English population. Its essence was a grand bargain in which the structure of the Church would be largely Roman Catholic in form, retaining hierarchy and, crucially, bishops (but with the monarch at the very apex, not the Bishop of Rome), while its services were mainly Protestant in character. This blessed blend not only kept domestic religious peace at the time but has continued for centuries.

In retrospect, this was an unduly rosy historical perspective. As a matter of faith, this shotgun marriage between two rival views of God was a most curious creature. Whether one thinks of it as 'Cathotant' or 'Protolic', it was the first choice of virtually no one who took religion seriously. It caused deep fissures within the Church itself from the outset. Elizabeth had assumed that the overwhelming majority of those who had been priests under Mary would accept the new system and was stunned when it turned out that they were rather more principled. Many senior figures in the Church did not care for it at all, and one Archbishop of Canterbury, Edmund Grindal, was essentially suspended from his position because he was openly dismissive of the new order. Most people who were focused on these matters thought that the 1559 settlement was, at best, a holding operation. Perhaps the sole individual who defended the new regime in full was Elizabeth as supreme governor.

The cracks really began to show within a decade. At first, those still inclined towards the old faith were allowed to pay lip service to the settlement, while how they might pray privately was up to them. This was the Elizabeth who had no wish for 'a window on men's souls'. After the uprising of the northern nobility in 1569 and an influx of Roman Catholic missionaries from abroad, the queen took rather more interest in opening the curtains on what her flock really thought about religion, and their obedience became obligatory while discreet Catholicism was deemed to be the prelude to treason.

There might have been a national security case for this change in attitude. It is harder to justify why those who wanted a Protestant Church more firmly rooted in Lutheranism or better still Calvinism faced a form of persecution as well. The Puritans, unlike the Roman Catholics who could look to Mary, Queen of Scots, had no rival to Elizabeth whom they aspired to place upon her throne instead. Elizabeth, although not particularly taken by the finer points of doctrine, would not budge an inch. It was her Church, so she should be in command of it. John Whitgift, as Archbishop of Canterbury, an able theologian, did his best to paper over the cracks by adding more ballast to Church teaching, but he was assailed by those of an Anglo-Catholic hue, or of a neo-Calvinist bent, or the queen.

As would hold for many instances under Elizabeth I, she had created a potential powder keg in this sphere. It would not detonate during her tenure but would be more testing for others to defuse later. The Elizabethan settlement averted a choice between apples and oranges in favour of fruit salad. Religion was far too important a force in life for this to satisfy the dietary requirements of faith. It was a settlement, if that is the right term for it at all, erected on sand. She was a rare advocate of it.

The final misrepresentation which must be corrected concerns the English victory over the Armada. The Spanish fleet was a mortal threat to the kingdom and Elizabeth's stirring words to her troops at Tilbury in 1588 are among the most memorable sentences that any monarch has ever delivered. That she was articulate and brave is self-evident, but what happened was less an English win than a Spanish loss.

There were two logical means by which Philip II and his absolutely huge fleet might invade England. The first would rely on sea power and involve the direct transportation of his fighting men from Spain to land somewhere on the English coastline. The second would shorten the distance involved by ferrying the large army that he already had in the Netherlands across the Channel. The strategy which he settled on – sending his navy around to the Low Countries to pick up his army there – was complicated to the verge of crackpot. Too many things could too easily go badly wrong.

It might have stood an outside chance of triumph if the weather had been better. It was atrocious. It allowed the English fleet to harry the Spanish navy into open sea in conditions that did not permit them to disembark in England, the Netherlands or, as an extreme Plan C, in Ireland either. It was the wind and the rain, not Sir Walter Raleigh or Sir Francis Drake, that was decisive. If Richard III needed a horse at the Battle of Bosworth Field in 1485, what Philip II lacked in 1588 was a meteorologist.

There is one last aspect to this tale that should be highlighted, if only because our English history has chosen to airbrush it out of its accounts of this period. A year after the failure of the Armada, a vast English taskforce, an English Armada or a Counter Armada, it could be said, involving over 150 ships and 23,375 men, led by the ordinarily resourceful Sir Francis Drake, headed to the Iberian Peninsula. The object was not outright conquest – that would have been far too audacious – but to inflict serious damage on Spain and Portugal. It was mayhem. Some forty ships were sunk or seized, and more than 10,000 men were killed or wounded, or died of disease. Philip regained his mastery of the waters.

All of this serves to provide some context for assessing how Elizabeth I measures within monarchy.

Professional Standing

The reviews of Elizabeth from her contemporary peers are a strikingly mixed bag. She certainly had her admirers and was deemed at her best when the chips were seriously down, as in the mid-1580s. She also had a host of critics and sceptics when it came to the management of her administration.

The first complaint was that, like Henry VIII, she was patently not interested in this area. She enjoyed the magical and mystical elements of monarchy but not the mundane details of government. She was an unmovable conservative, in that she hated change. She preferred to allow her trusted people to handle the paperwork. She tended to avoid meetings of the Privy Council, which she insisted should be small in terms of its membership but massive in the range of questions that it addressed. There were, it should be stated, some significant and impressive innovations in local government at the end of her reign, but she was not only not responsible for this, she probably barely noticed it.

The second was her tendency to accumulate favourites — invariably dashing men — and promote them excessively, irrespective of whether their talents matched the task in hand. Robert Dudley, whom she ennobled as Earl of Leicester, was the main beneficiary of this trait at the beginning of her time, while the Earl of Essex, the stepson of Dudley, was the man of the hour later on (until they fell out, he conspired, and she had him executed). These favourites would clash with more qualified figures such as William Cecil (Lord Burghley) and later his son Robert. This undermined policy.

To round things off there was her temperament. She could be inconsistent, inconsiderate and indecisive. Orders would be issued which would have to be retracted later due to impracticality. She was a presence to behold but on her own terms. The quality of government would steadily decline.

Public Opinion

Elizabeth started her tenure basking in stratospheric approval. It was useful not to be Mary Tudor. The burning of Protestant martyrs met with very intense national disapproval. The sense that Spain had really been running the show, with the absent King Philip II a figure of displeasure to most people, was also an asset to the new incumbent. News of her ascension was the cause of the sixteenth-century version of street parties. Her coronation attracted staggering numbers to watch it. She milked this utterly shamelessly and deployed the 'I am, like you, English through and through' card for all it was worth. In her entire time as queen, she took the chance to be seen by ordinary people and even mingle with them (the royal walkabout was not invented in the age of the second Elizabeth). She surely had a second spike in popular appreciation after the defeat of the Armada ended the fear of an invasion.

She would not, however, have been popular with everyone. The Roman Catholic community, much of which was instinctively loyal to her, would not have appreciated its enforced ostracisation. Puritans, as noted, had their own grounds for grievance. Mainstream men and women would have become aware that the queen was ever more reliant on the network of spies organised by Lord Walsingham and perhaps felt uneasy about their activities. There were many years of hardship for the poor. Her indifference to public administration was a blind spot which had implications for the lesser orders.

Those who had the most cause for complaint were in Ireland. An uneasy accord between the 'Old Irish' and the 'Old English' was shattered by the importation of a 'New English' population. The queen was a control freak and not too fussed about what needed to be done to maintain control. There were numerous incidents of indiscriminate slaughter right across the Emerald Isle, many still recalled there more than five centuries later. It was a vengeance of a sort with no parallel in Britain. Elizabeth may still have held sway with most of the English in 1600. She was loathed by many Irish.

Financial Competence

Even those who would be inclined to award Elizabeth the benefit of the doubt elsewhere would have to concede that the management of financial affairs in her time was a car crash before automobiles had been invented. There is virtually nothing that can be said in mitigation. It was incredibly inept.

Henry VIII had left behind a rough-and-ready means of war taxation in the form of subsidies. Mary handed on taxes on foreign trade (customs) which were also of value in putting money in the coffers. As Elizabeth did not much care for calling parliaments to raise taxation by that means (they often did so, but linked their largesse to the marriage, absence of, matter), it would have been in her interest to have developed these income streams further. By contrast, due to lack of attention they withered.

This had a devastating effect on income. Nobles had become adept at tax avoidance. Many families would insist that they were less wealthy at the end of her reign than they had been at the start of it. This was inconceivable. The Tudor state was one of the largest in Europe but run on a shoestring.

This had some extremely undesirable knock-on effects. Public servants were paid a pittance. To make ends meet they engaged in theft, misrepresentation of expenses and outright corruption, charging the public over the odds to inflate their salaries. Always allergic to change, Elizabeth awarded Crown offices for life, which meant the burnt-out and the bent could not be sidelined. As complaints were made about conditions even at the highest levels (outrageously in the light of private profiteering), concessions were offered in the form of monopolies and patents instead of formal salary increases. This would prove a distortion of the market, undercutting the efficient practice of trade policies.

It meant that there were few monuments to the Elizabethan era. It has been estimated while she spent around a tenth of what her father had done on buildings, she had to sell six of her palaces. Asset disposals of this sort were only one of a number of improvised measures to find money. Land was also put under the hammer. Bills went unpaid. Borrowing escalated. Fiscal farce hit its height when captains were expected to settle the running costs of their own ships (even in combat) and colonels were informed that they would have to assist with the upkeep of their regiments. In an example which could only be imagined in *Monty Python's Flying Circus* or *Mr Bean*, it is seriously suggested that at the siege of Edinburgh Castle in 1573, soldiers were instructed to approach the walls and retrieve the cannonballs that had already been shot so that they could be recycled and blasted again. If the Armada had managed to land, it is not obvious what the English would have done about it. Elizabeth might not have been an accountant like Henry VII, but she bore final responsibility for this.

Foreign Policy

Elizabeth had to be imaginative in foreign policy and there were times when she was exactly that. The broader political landscape across the European continent was changing and more complex. She built up the Navy with all the resources she could acquire, but chronic cash-flow problems were an impediment.

At the beginning of her reign, France was still perceived as England's leading opponent. The loss of Calais had been as painful for Elizabeth after the event as it was for Mary when it happened. It could not be accepted lying down. An additional concern was that Scotland was firmly in the grip of France, with Mary, Queen of Scots (the recent widow of Francis II of France), entirely content to be its client. The bigger picture was not a novelty, but the standard course of action had been to establish closer relations with Spain as a counterbalance to French machinations. Religion, and Elizabeth's distaste for considering her former half brother-in-law Philip II as her suitor, threw a spanner in the works. But as long as Elizabeth did not actively aspire to export the Protestant faith, Spain was amenable.

The initial Elizabethan foray abroad was therefore, in 1562–63, to snatch Le Havre and then use it to compel an exchange which would restore Calais to English sovereignty. It did not work, and it burnt money. England withdrew from continental enterprises for the better part of two decades. In the intervening years, there were a number of dramatic developments. France was engulfed in a combination of dynastic disputes and conflicts related (but not confined) to religious affiliation. This was of assistance to Elizabeth as Paris could not be a menace while so internally divided. Far more of a worry was that Philip II was flexing his muscles in the Netherlands and suppressing the Protestants. This opened the door to large numbers of his troops being stationed not far away from England. One reaction to this was a part privatisation of foreign policy in the shape of state-sponsored piracy, with ships aligned to Elizabeth attacking Spanish interests in the Atlantic and Caribbean, but without the English emblem being entirely attached to their antics. Philip II became increasingly irked by this.

With some considerable reluctance, Elizabeth accepted that she had to intervene in the Netherlands. This became official doctrine through the Treaty of Nonsuch in 1585. The Earl of Leicester (for whom she still held a candle) was sent off to be her envoy. He overpromised, she underdelivered. The Dutch would have accepted her as their queen if she had pulled out all the stops for them. Elizabeth (and there is a cynical merit in what she did) knowingly pulled out only half those stops. She wanted to do enough to prevent Philip II winning in the Netherlands but not so much that, riled, he lost there.

After the Armada there was one last attempt at finishing where the monarch had started. The scales had tipped in favour of Henry of Navarre (to become Henry IV) in the fratricidal French schism. He was the best bet for England in terms of a more productive dialogue with France and against Spain. It made sense to send an expeditionary force to be linked with his forthcoming victory and win favour.

With the Earl of Leicester now dead, the emerging new favourite, the Earl of Essex, was charged with mobilising military support in France in 1589 and 1591. This fared no better than it had in 1562–63. England aimed to assist Henry in the siege of Rouen. This had to be abandoned. These troops then traipsed around northern France in search of something to do, before coming home without glory. With money once again minuscule, this was the end of the road for activist Elizabethan foreign policy. It would be unreasonable to dismiss its overall record; England did, after all, retain its independence and much of what Elizabeth wanted to achieve was accomplished. Yet it was all rather haphazard.

Succession

As established earlier, Elizabeth took a reckless approach towards the issue of succession. England avoided a meltdown, potentially its own civil turmoil or war of religion, because she did not die at a time when the uncertainty over who would come after her would have been extremely inconvenient. A relatively smooth transfer of authority between the late queen and James VI of Scotland did occur but mostly because of a coded conversation conducted by Robert Cecil with the Scottish monarch, not through a belated realisation by Elizabeth that she was not immortal and that her subjects had to have far more certainty than she had been willing to consider. It could all have been far worse. It was no thanks to her that it was not. Her performance on succession should mightily stain her reputation.

For all these reasons, Elizabeth, despite her association with Shakespeare and the other giant talents of her time, has to be ranked as overrated. Her virtues were at least matched by her vices. One last point should be made about her. Napoleon asked of his generals, 'Are they lucky?'[7] Elizabeth was lucky.

---

7   *Oxford Essential Quotations* (6th edition), edited by Susan Ratcliffe (2018).

William III (1689–1702)

OVERRATED

History, the eminent scholar Norman Davies observed, is written by both winners and losers, but it is invariably the version of it framed by the winners that shapes the narrative the most. This tendency may explain why the reputation of William III or William of Orange is somewhat higher than a more neutral and nuanced assessment of his reign would lead one to conclude. He is portrayed as a heroic individual, invited to England on behalf of the representatives of its people (at best, half-true), to act for 'liberty' against 'tyranny' (not true), who came to share the throne with his wife Mary (who had a respectable claim in the circumstances of 1689 to be the sole contender for monarchy) after his father-in-law James II was deemed to have abdicated (he had not) and who then continued as king after his wife died young in 1694 (legal but stretching legitimacy somewhat). He thus embodies the 'Glorious Revolution', an achievement that on its own implies greatness (to be discussed here).

William was certainly an intriguing figure. He was the only child of William II, Prince of Orange and Stadtholder of much of Holland, and his wife Mary, thze Princess Royal, eldest daughter of Charles I. His father died of smallpox a week before he was born, and his mother then treated him with little interest (losing a parent early or being neglected is a running theme in analysing British monarchs). His primary aim as a young man was to reassert his hereditary right to be recognised as Stadtholder as a number of provinces had preferred to put that post into a holding slot rather than hand it to an infant with all the complexities of determining regency for what would be a lengthy period of time. His foes in this were other anti-Orange factions inside the Dutch nobility and, at a distance, France.

Allowing for blood ties, his ally, and a potentially pivotal one, should have been England. Although the political big brother of his country, England could not be relied on. This was the case under Oliver Cromwell and the Commonwealth when, despite religious kinship, commercial rivalries led to the First Anglo-Dutch War. The restoration of Charles II (William's uncle) should have made matters easier, but that king spoke out of two sides of his mouth when it came to Holland, publicly on side, but privately cutting a deal with Louis XIV of France in the secret Treaty of Dover of 1670, which would have seen France take over Holland as a vassal state, with William offered an upgrade of title but token power. This led to the Second Anglo-Dutch War and then a third one. At one stage, in 1672, it did look as if Holland might be overrun by French forces, which had the side effect, clearly welcome at his end, that resistance to making the then 22-year-old William the ÷ necessarily disappeared.

The Dutch were strong enough in combat to fight matters to an advantageous standstill. France could not impose itself on the Dutch people. William's status at home and abroad rose as a result. Charles II then engaged in another diplomatic volte-face and strongly urged William to marry Mary, eldest daughter of James, Duke of York, heir presumptive to the king himself. James was not as keen on the proposal but ultimately did not resist as his higher priority was producing a male heir by his second wife (the Roman

William III (1689–1702)

Catholic, as James now openly was himself, Mary of Modena). The wedding of William III and Mary took place in 1677 and he became a potentially vital player in English politics thereafter.

There are three events which frame the context of William's reign and which are essential to appreciate before applying the five measures or metrics of monarchy to him. They are: what occurred from 1685 to 1689 and the means by which William became king (to begin with in a shared context with Mary); the provisions of the Bill of Rights and other legislation that would constrain both William and all future monarchs, which he accepted without much protest because his attention was elsewhere; and the Act of Settlement (1701), which was caused to a sizeable degree by the fact that he would not take another wife after the death of Mary II, which if that union had resulted in a child might have avoided a succession crisis, although it would have meant twisting bloodline monarchy to a further extent.

The 'Glorious Revolution' is a term which is open to discussion. The convulsions of 1685–89 were sensational. James ascended to the throne on the death of his brother in 1685 with less strife than might have been anticipated, considering that a large slice of Parliament had wanted legally to exclude him because of his religion. An uprising against him in Scotland was quashed without much effort (there was still a horde of Catholic sympathisers there) and the rebellion headed by the Duke of Monmouth (illegitimate son of Charles II) in the West Country was almost comically inept and saw the duke himself executed more or less on the spot, and then an exceptionally harsh crackdown on anyone thought to have sympathised with his cause (the infamous Bloody Assizes under Judge Jeffreys).

Overreading what all this meant for his authority, James then set about attempting to undermine the anti-Catholic Test Acts by amending, reinterpreting or simply ignoring their provisions, in the cause of religious tolerance, both towards his own co-religionists and (which is critical in the 'liberty' versus 'tyranny' thesis) towards nonconformist Protestants as well. This may have been entirely tactical by James, but it makes the notion that he was hell bent on a Mary Tudor-style reconversion of England (which he would not have stood a chance of implementing, as he knew) an idea without credence. James started to make appointments of Roman Catholics to various portfolios, which was obviously at odds with the Test Acts, and issued two different Declarations of Indulgence. In a fatal mistake (and probably a needless one), he asserted that Anglican clergy had to read them to their followers.

What might have been a containable contest of wills spun out of control. In the summer of 1688, the Archbishop of Canterbury and six other bishops urged the king to withdraw the second Declaration of Indulgence, which he declined to do, stating that they should be put on trial for seditious libel (at least he followed a form of due process). They were acquitted, a verdict which was celebrated.

James II attempted during these three years to persuade Mary and William (in that order) to come out in support of his drive for religious tolerance. They would not do so. This was a stumbling block of some importance as Mary was the heir apparent. All that was upended on 10 June 1688, when it was announced that Mary of Modena, who had endured ten failed pregnancies, had given birth to a healthy son to be called James. Protestant propagandists put it about that this was a subterfuge, but there is no evidence to suggest this was correct. The route to the succession of a string of Catholic kings standing off against a Protestant Establishment and Parliament was suddenly now wide open.

Enter William. The Bishop of London and six lay persons of status (the 'Immortal Seven') sought out William and asserted that he should intervene and place his wife on the throne. He did not need very much encouragement but was not enticed by the charitable notion that he should acquire no benefit of his own. He had been planning for such an opening for months and a very large collection of Dutch ships (more than 450), sailors and soldiers (around 40,000 in total) landed unopposed at Brixham in what was, fundamentally, a conquest or an invasion and not some version of a peacekeeping effort.

James could not drum up support to resist what his son-in-law was scheming, usurpation. He had no survival plan so initially aspired to flee to France, but he was captured and returned to William who let him escape abroad (as the alternative, realistically, was executing him, which was very unattractive). James was predominantly the author of his own misfortunes. He should have been more patient and more subtle in the pursuit of religious tolerance. The camp of 'tyrant' is not, though, one into which he properly falls, and that he was irked by the part played in his downfall by his son-in-law is not surprising.

The second seminal dimension lies in what happened constitutionally in the aftermath. In early 1689, Parliament convened to add some belated legal cover to what had happened without it. Many felt that Mary II should be queen in the full sense of that term and William a superior version of consort. Historic memories of the incredibly unpopular joint rule of Philip II of Spain and the first Mary would have served as a disincentive to engage in anything like a repeated version of that innovation.

William would not accept that outcome. At a minimum, he wished to be co-monarch. If not, then he would head back to Holland and his wife made it plain that she would go with him and not take up the throne in her own unique right. This was blackmail, but William was well placed for extortion.

He had his way. The awkward architecture of a shared monarchy (but with him in the driving seat on a day-to-day basis) was rapidly constructed. Initially it was not set out what would happen if one or other of the two monarchs expired (it was the death of Mary, not William, that would be a challenge), but by the end of 1689, this was resolved with the rule that at the death of one, the other stayed on. This was making-it-up-as-we-go-along territory, but it offered security to the novel political order.

If William had won that battle, Parliament would triumph in the broader war. As part of the compact by which William would sit on the throne, despite not having the best blood claim to it, he would agree to what was initially called a Declaration of Rights but then became a grander-sounding Bill of Rights. This repeated the falsehood and fantasy that James II had abandoned his kingdom and inserted an array of new restrictions on monarchical authority. The strength of William's hand was such that if he had been minded, he could have pushed back on some clauses, but he did not. His thinking was at least as much about Holland as it was England, and his concentration was upon France and Louis XIV and what he could do with England's Crown in that competition, which would consume his whole life.

The Bill of Rights was not the only measure which would bind him. An Act of Indulgence gave more freedom to nonconformists as Parliament finally realised that fighting on two fronts over matters of religion was restrictive. The Triennial Act of 1694 ensured that Parliament would legally have to be called at least once every three years (a major irritation for monarchs). The Mutiny Act of 1689 meant that no standing army could be called in peacetime without the backing of the House of Commons. A Civil List Act in 1698 extended parliamentary command over the finances of the king. Even the creation of the Bank of England in 1694 could be viewed as clipping the wings of the House of Stuart. William remained the only king that the Protestant elite had, and James II was restive in France (having lost out on the chance to reclaim his throne at the Battle of the Boyne in 1690) and he had a son to boot. King William was disinclined to resist Parliament not because he was instinctively a democrat of any kind, but because it was all a distraction. The death of Mary, from smallpox, in 1694 meant that he ruled alone for the remainder of his tenure, even though it could be argued that this diluted his legitimacy.

The final factor of scale which creates the contours of William's reign flowed from this. He and Mary had no children (nor was there much to suggest any effort to do so from 1678 onwards). Having bent the rules once to allow for a co-monarchy, and then again in 1694 to permit him to continue ruling even though his sister-in-law Anne had a strong case for coming after Mary, there is not much doubt that, if William had agreed to marry again and then had a child of his own (especially if it were male), then Parliament would have let such a child (William IV?) become the heir apparent (the Bill of Rights of 1689 explicitly opened this route to the throne). William showed no interest in doing so. This did not matter while Anne had a surviving son, but when he died in 1700 matters became explosive.

The end result was the Act of Settlement of 1701. Parliament dropped any pretence at traditional bloodlines and instead placed the Protestant religion at the heart of its calculations. William had not left it with much other choice. No fewer than fifty-seven individuals with a stronger argument for themselves on the basis of blood were passed over because they were Roman Catholics or married to Roman Catholics or, in a few strange instances, Parliament did not care for them irrespective of their Protestant faith, in favour of Sophia, the Electress of Hanover, and those who came after (she helpfully had six sons). That her eldest – the future George I – was something of a psychopath and spoke no English was immaterial. He was willing to be an Anglican (when in England). William could have avoided this.

He did not. It is one of the reasons why the five measurements of monarchy do not fit him well.

Professional Standing

The professional standing of William III could not avoid being a contentious matter. The conditions in which he took the throne had a seismic impact on perceptions of him. If you were a High Tory who disapproved of the removal of James II, then nothing the new king did was destined to change your assessment of him. If you were slightly more flexible than that but deemed Mary to be the rightful heir to James II, then William's campaign to make himself the co-monarch and within that structure very much the first among equals is inherently a black mark against him. The bulk of those whose opinions counted were not in either of these contingents and wanted to see the best in their king.

This would not always be straightforward. Having all but thrown his toys out of the pram to be made a co-monarch, William then spent a lot of time overseas either in his original jurisdiction of Holland or in military contests with the France of Louis XIV. While he was an absentee landlord, it would be Mary II who exercised the functions of the monarchy, but she was not suited by temperament to throw her weight around with Parliament, so instead William engaged in an inconsistent micromanagement in which he attempted to conduct the affairs of state while often seated on horseback elsewhere.

His conundrum was that he had no band of supporters who satisfied all aspects of his agenda. The Tories were the most ambivalent about the fact that he was there at all (they saw the despatch of James II as a regrettable obligation), but on the other hand they inclined towards being anti-French and willing to fund William's military ambitions in that quarter. The Whigs were much more solid in their endorsement of William and content to see him be more than a nominal co-monarch, but they were the leading faction which would push through laws and changes that limited the monarch and were more sceptical in the cost–benefit analysis of fighting the French. In so far as these parties could contest elections in which it was entirely clear who was wearing which colours, the Tories were at the helm after the hustings of 1690 and the Whigs once those of 1695 had been conducted. It did not matter much which side had the upper hand; William's interest in domestic affairs beyond that of national security was slight, and Mary seems to have had few forceful opinions of her own either. Whether or not William might have been a shrewd public administrator would never be fully tested.

This was far more of a complication for national life after Mary had died in 1694 and as it became self-evident that William would not be taking a second wife (there has been a deliberation among certain historians as to whether there were homosexual inclinations which might have been at the root of all this, but while he had male favourites, the jury is out on this subject and will surely remain absent). The king did not become any more intrigued by the country of which he was from Mary's death the sole adopted monarch, and Parliament did not protest very much about his apparent disinclinations. He remained a massive barrier to any Jacobite comeback and after an abortive plot to assassinate William by Catholic conspirators in 1696, as long as he fulfilled that role he would not be challenged. His professional standing stayed in the eye of the beholder. The politics of his age entrenched views.

Public Opinion

If William looked on his subjects with something of a sense of detachment, the same could be said about how the public regarded him. Partisanship on the drama of 1688 and 1689 coloured opinions here as well. Catholic Englishmen probably never accepted him. The Scots did not necessarily want a Dutchman as their monarch (even some staunchly Protestant people in Scotland were not content). This would be compounded by William's perceived stance on the Massacre of Glencoe (1692) and more surreally by him being blamed for the failure of the Darien scheme, an outlandish get-rich-quick scheme funded by Scottish investors to establish a colony in the Isthmus of Panama in 1698, which had to be abandoned in 1700 with staggering losses for those who had put up the money (much of Lowland Scotland had signed up for this barking-mad plan). The Scottish nobility involved wanted to be bailed out of their troubles, but the king and Parliament only put forward partial compensation.

In Ireland, those Catholics who might have been agnostic about him when he arrived on the scene (and there were not very many of those) would have hardened their dislike after the treatment that was handed out to Roman Catholics in the wake of William's victory at the Battle of the Boyne.

Mary II does seem to have assumed plausible popularity. Her right to be queen in the showdown of 1688–89 was acknowledged even if this involved sanctioning a daughter pushing a father out (but those with a longer sense of English history would have conceded that having the offspring or wives of monarchs colluding to depose the king of the day was hardly unprecedented). A position where William was abroad, and Mary was seen to be exercising the prerogatives of the monarch, may well have been an acceptable compromise as far as mass sentiment went, even if anyone remotely close to the government would have been able to tell that she was no more than a puppet of the king.

When she died (William would lose his father before being born, his mother when he was 10 years old, and his wife five years into their collective tenure, all to smallpox – if only Edward Jenner had been born a century earlier), it is recorded that the mourning for her was impressive. Whether this was because she truly had the popular touch, or because her disappearance meant that a foreigner was to be the monarch of England, Scotland and Ireland without the fig leaf that he was only half in charge, could be disputed. It clearly took the constitution into uncharted waters. If Anne had been motivated to make more noise about her rights being compromised by the terms of the Bill of Rights, then there could have been fireworks, but she was willing to bide her time (and must have been confident that, if she could avoid a fatal outbreak of smallpox, that hour would come eventually). The end of Mary II would take away a protective shield in terms of public opinion for William and that weakened him.

To be blunt, he probably did not care. He was never considered to be a congenial king because he made very little effort to endear himself to English sympathies. He was there not to be James II (or the menace of James III), rather than to be privately regarded with reverence. England was there vastly to increase his options in dealing with France. His liaison with the English was an arranged marriage.

His popularity did decrease from 1694 onwards but not to the extent that it was a threat to him. He actually gained a spike in support in 1696 when the Catholic plan to kill him was revealed, as it was a salutary reminder to those who found it hard to cheer at his reign of whether they would prefer an alternative. This state of consensus could not be continued. His standing would shrink again (as will be described) as a result of the economic malaise of the late 1690s, which struck ordinary people hard, and war-weariness even among those who disliked France intensely. He would die unloved in 1702.

Financial Competence

The changes which William had accepted, such as the invention of the Bank of England in 1694 and the formation of the Civil List (worth £700,000 to him, a very respectable sum) in 1698, meant that he did not have the sovereignty over public finances and the wider condition of the economy that many of those who had come before him did. He was not, however, an irrelevant figure either. He could undertake activities which were more or less expensive (particularly warfare) and this would have knock-on effects that the proverbial man in the English street would become all too aware of.

Unfortunately, if such a man was attuned to the impact of Williamomics, then the odds are that he would not be a pleased person. The wars with France and a general sense of a less than competent Treasury made the 1690s an unsatisfactory decade. The conflict with France which fixated the king was a crushing burden on others. This was a time of runaway inflation, and the fighting would be a liability to maritime trade, which would in other circumstances have been expected to deliver up prosperity. Taxation had to double in order to set the coffers something close to straight, which went down as badly then as would have been the situation in England 300-plus years later.

This was not merely a recession. It went deeper than that. There is evidence that times were so hard that actual hunger was recorded in parts of the country. England has very rarely had cause to worry about famine, and if it had, it would be due to diabolic weather conditions, not a managerial mishap. Others could tell that the economy was vulnerable, and the speculators enjoyed a field day. The value of the currency depreciated rapidly between 1695 and 1697, which constituted an all-out crisis. The embryonic Bank of England was nearly knocked over before it had the opportunity to start business. Matters improved a little in the last five years of William's reign but were still starkly unenchanting. He may have been a good soldier (although historians debate this). He was a terrible accountant.

Foreign Policy

As implied continuously through this account, William's first, second and third priority was France. At every opening he would collude against the interests of Louis XIV and compel England to do so. In the year that he took command (supposedly jointly) of the throne, the Holy Roman Empire and the Dutch had combined against France, so it was no shock at all that William steered his new nation into this Grand Alliance. There followed a nine-year war between 1688 and 1697 in which there were some English military successes for which William III would merit credit, but it was cripplingly costly. There would have been much relief when it concluded with the Treaty of Ryswick of 1697, which did reduce France's command of the European continent and allowed the economic malaise to be eased.

It would be a temporary interlude. An enormous difficulty loomed on the horizon. The King of Spain was physically impeded and would plainly die childless. The issue of who could come after him was a horror show. Either the Holy Roman Empire or, even worse, France would be the beneficiary of the most probable transitions. England (and Holland) would be a victim in terms of the power politics.

To be fair, William saw this coming and tried to conjure up a diplomatic solution which would limit the damage and avert Europe spending the first decade of the eighteenth century involved in a war which would almost certainly be of a scope that was even greater than the last decade of the seventeenth. There was a First Partition Treaty in 1698, which was disrupted when a key figure promptly died, and then a Second Partition Treaty in 1700, which might have done the trick had the dying King of Spain, Charles II, not disregarded its structures and come up with his own model that suited France.

In what turned out to be the last full year of his reign, William would ensure that England was dragged into the War of the Spanish Succession, which would last for thirteen years. This was not received with anything close to overwhelming backing within the country. To add petrol to this fire, France was now loudly championing the cause of James, son of James II (who had died in 1701, which was useful to the Jacobite cause as he was a polarising and, to many, discredited choice for a restoration). Thus, the succession question was ever sharper and the Act of Settlement a less than stellar answer.

For the third time in not much more than a century, England was about to adopt a formula for its own future which would involve an outsider, a foreigner, being imported, not because it was thought an ideal outcome but as it was the least bad option allowing for alternatives on the dynastic market.

Succession

William had been born into a succession crisis (over which he had zero control) and one might have thought this would make him more alert than most about the importance of avoiding leaving one behind. He was not. He had no children himself and did not appear to regard this as a dereliction of duty; after Mary's death, he did not remarry and allow himself a second bite of the breeding cherry. He gambled (in so far as he contemplated the scene at all) on his sister-in-law Anne providing some systemic salvation. He seems to have been at ease in delegating the Act of Settlement of 1701 to his parliamentarians.

This aptly summarises his tenure. William III was not a malevolent soul, although it is ironic that a man personally open-minded on religion would mine militant anti-Catholic attitudes as he did. He just was not aligned to England's interests sufficiently. This leaves him as a highly overrated monarch.

Anne (1702–14)

UNDERRATED

If ever there was a British monarch unfairly dismissed largely on their appearance, then it is Queen Anne. She is largely remembered (if much at all) for being plain, stout almost to the point of immobility (she had to be ferried around in a sedan chair), and for an astonishing number of failed pregnancies (the consensus number used to be seventeen, but nineteen is now in the frame). The fact that she was actually the inaugural British queen, at least of England and Scotland, rather than at the helm of those countries separately, is treated as an inconsequential detail. It was not. If compared to the three or four monarchs who went before her (Charles II, James II, William and Mary, then William III alone) and even more forcefully the four who came after (Georges I–IV), she was a splendid figure.

She did not have the easiest of upbringings. Her father, James II, was a philanderer of such fervour as to make her uncle, Charles II, appear almost chaste. Her mother was Anne Hyde, daughter of the 1st Earl of Clarendon. She was hardly a commoner, but it might have been thought that James would be married off to more suitable (ideally Protestant) continental

European royalty. This might well have been the case had Anne not been seven months pregnant (with the future Mary II). This was the House of Stuart version of a shotgun wedding. Charles II could see advantages in the match (but mostly for himself), so he encouraged it. In the circumstances, all concerned had little choice.

Domestic arrangements were complicated. Anne senior, initially secretly and then openly, became a Roman Catholic. This was slightly awkward for the monarchy as a whole, but manageable. When James, then the Duke of York, went in the same direction, that was much more destabilising. He was the heir apparent and there was little indication that Charles II would bring forth legitimate issue. The most committed Protestants did their best to drive James into exile and exclude him from the throne. They were effective in the former for a while, but not the latter. The young Anne did not see him much. Her mother died while she was a child. She seems to have got on well with Mary of Modena, her stepmother.

This may explain why she was more reticent and reluctant than her sister during the turmoil of 1688. While both were willing to believe (and indeed discussed the matter in letters) that the birth of their supposed half-brother James had somehow been faked, Anne clearly felt more guilty at being party to a conspiracy to depose her father as king. She may have been closer to him or more inclined to see blood as more important that religious doctrine, but she was very much in 'sorrow, not anger' mode. She had less to obtain personally from the arrangement than her sister and brother-in-law. There was still a chance, after all, that they would not only win the throne but then produce an heir.

The relationship between the two sisters from 1689 to 1694 was a delicate one. Mary and Anne had disputes over Anne's status (should she be treated as the heir apparent or not), her accommodation (how grand a palace), her broader financial position (Anne wanted, and in the end obtained, her own allowance from Parliament), what part her husband (Prince George of Denmark) should play in national life and, most bitterly, her very close friendship with Sarah Churchill and her husband John Churchill. Mary did not care for Sarah on a personal level. William III had doubts about the loyalty of John Churchill (in 1692 these reached a level which involved sending him to the Tower of London).

The death of Mary II in 1694 prompted what was at best a partial reconciliation. Anne looked more like the heir apparent (although if William remarried and produced children she would cease to be) and this was reflected in where she lived, the size of her retinue and the resources she was offered. There were still tensions. She lobbied for a meaningful post for her husband, but he stayed a fringe player. William did not want her to see state papers. She was not made regent in his many absences. She could have been better prepared for her duties than she was. This was hardly her tardiness.

There were three huge events (two much better recalled than the other) which framed Anne's reign. One was domestic politics (the Act of Union). The second was foreign affairs (the War of the Spanish Succession). The final one was an external shock – the Great Frost of 1709 – and its social and economic impact.

England and Scotland had since 1603 shared a monarch but not an enormous amount else. This was a compact which Scotland felt entitled to be discontent with. Its king (or queen) was always out of the country. The methods devised to deal with this were frequently unsatisfactory. This might have been more tolerable if there had been automatic access to England's lucrative wealth, but that did not materialise either. Alienation plus a significant Roman Catholic minority meant that there was a constituency which could be tempted by the idea of an independent choice of monarch (possibly James III).

William had sought to stimulate English interest in appeasing this with a favourable Act of Union. He did not press it hard and made very little progress. Anne came at the subject with more intensity. In her first speech to Parliament as monarch, she referred to an Act of Union as 'very necessary'. The Scottish Parliament then passed the Act of Security in 1703, which recognised Anne as queen but did not provide a pledge to follow the Act of Settlement thereafter. A pointed amendment was added to it which made the future backing of Scotland for the English Crown contingent on free trade. Anne would not sign the legislation until that clause had been removed, but it was a shot across her bows.

It stoked urgency. There seemed to be a small window of opportunity during which the English elite had an incentive to take an Act of Union seriously (the mass public in England had little zeal for the idea and tended to treat the Scots as barbarians), while Scotland might accept an enticing offer. It was Anne's camp who pressed the importance of a bargain. She was by far the primary cheerleader for it.

This was not the most comfortable accord to conjure up. England would have to put a lot of money on the table, not just in terms of opening up commercial markets which had been closed (what was being proposed was the largest free trade area in Europe) but in restructuring the national debt in a form that would be attractive to Scotland. The Scots were signing away their birthright in return. An autonomous monarchy (even if it had been pooled with England for a century) that had been there for centuries would probably end, in favour of an obscure set from Hanover with no connection to Scotland at all (after a tenure of the House of Stuart since 1381) and a Parliament would be closed.

The pact was not an unfair one. Scotland won free trade within the terms of the Navigation Acts. It did lose its Parliament but retained much of its own law, its municipal corporations and its currency, and the Church of Scotland remained an institution of its own, not an outpost of the Church of England.

Anne (1702–14)

The country would send forty-five MPs to Westminster and sixteen peers entered the House of Lords. It meant Anne was Queen of Great Britain. At the signing ceremony for the legislation in Parliament, she asserted: 'I consider this Union as a matter of the greatest importance to the wealth, strength and safety of the whole island.'[8] She was probably among a small minority who felt like that.

The Act was controversial within Scotland. Accusations that it had been obtained by crude bribery did not take long to be aired. The Duke of Hamilton, who had been its main advocate north of the border, was vilified. Jacobite sympathies were stoked. It would not be accepted universally. At no stage in the last 300 years or so has it satisfied everyone in Scotland. In the last two decades, this has manifested itself in the strength of the Scottish National Party in the devolved Parliament that was restored in 1999, by an independence referendum in 2014 that was hotly contested and showed the enduring aspiration of many Scots to be shot of the Act of Union once and for all. It was not, in its opening phase, much cared for by the English either. An English- (not Scottish)-motivated motion debated in the House of Lords in 1713 to abandon the Act of Union fell short by a single vote.

It would be churlish, nonetheless, not to concede that the Act of Union 1707 is an incredibly significant piece of legislation in English and Scottish history. Fat, frumpy Anne championed it.

If binding England and Scotland together in a bond was her domestic goal, then the prosecution of the War of the Spanish Succession (1701–03) would cast a giant shadow over her period as queen. It was not a conflict of her choosing – William III had bequeathed this – and while it would have been all but impossible for England and Scotland (later Great Britain) to have sat it out (in the worst-case scenario, a complete French triumph,

---

[8] Norman Davies, *The Isles: A History* (1999), p. 527.

the arrival of James 'the Old Pretender' as king was possible), the extent and the means by which the country intervened in the continental affray was contentious.

The dominance of the conflict was overwhelming. It was made far more challenging for Anne as her gender (and her health) meant that the notion that she should make an appearance at a battlefield was incredible. The monarchy as an institution had to hand over what could be argued was its single most fundamental function, the security of the realm, entirely to others. The principal 'other' was John Churchill, who had been such a close confidant of the queen due to her partnership with Sarah, his wife, but as the first decade of the eighteenth century went on, what had been an asset became a stark liability.

The war had its pluses and its minuses. The pluses were that it brought some spectacular victories in the heart of Europe which pumped up patriotic pride and fervour. The rout at Blenheim in 1704 (an event of such prominence that Anne made her commander the Duke of Marlborough), a similar win at Ramillies in 1706, a daring strategy at Oudenarde in 1708, a piece of military genius at Malplaquet in 1709, and after that engineering a surrender at Bouchain in 1711, sharpened a sense of invincibility. Marlborough had a status as a military commander that was unchallenged and admired in his era.

Not by everyone at home, however. Many Tories would have wanted to see the fight occur at sea. Naval power was a sunk cost (paradoxically), whereas Marlborough's determination to fight on land was a relative novelty and involved considerably more current expenditure. What is more, truly extraordinary as his many victories were, they did not bring the end of the campaign any closer. They altered the balance of power on the continent, but they were not a knock-out blow. They could not dodge the unfortunate reality that the next King of Spain would be a person with a tie either to France or to the Holy Roman Empire. Even if Britain had been able to defeat absolutely all comers and march on Madrid, it would not have been able to insert a candidate of its own as King of Spain. As the Act of Settlement had made all too plain, it was finding it difficult enough to identify a successor to Anne.

Yet Marlborough wanted to extend this mostly unpopular and perpetual war to some kind of finale. If Anne aspired differently, out of either principle or exhaustion, she would have to work around him.

Finally, the economic distress that flowed from the War of the Spanish Succession would be made far more distressing by an act of nature which until the Covid-19 pandemic had been forgotten.

Anne and the nation had been struck by one disaster early in her reign, when the Great Storm of 1703 had caused death and destruction (mostly through flooding) on land and created carnage for ships at sea. It would dislocate the economy severely. This turned out to be almost harmless when the Great Frost of 1709 materialised. People and livestock froze to death in unprecedented numbers (this was the time of 'the little ice age' when winters were generally exceptionally cold). Ordinary commerce was impractical. The economy might well have shrunk by the equivalent of 13 per cent in a year (a Bank of England analysis in 2020 suggested that the pandemic could have about the same effect, reviving awareness of the Great Frost for a short while) and it took several years to make up the losses.

It also seems to have been the catalyst for unrest on several fronts. The state of the Anglican Church had become a matter of debate, with a Tory clergyman called Henry Sacheverell obtaining acclaim at a trial by denouncing the Whigs for their approach to it (he was found guilty, but the queen and others connived to ensure that he received a token sentence). Economic dissatisfaction led to agitation and, on some occasions, outright violence. The military had to be deployed on home soil.

The Riot Act of 1714 was enacted to contain the incitement. The costly war was even more of a ball and chain. This was not a happy time to be king or queen. It fell to Anne to find some solutions to the conundrum.

With that in mind, how she fared should be tested against the five metrics of monarchy.

Professional Standing

Anne has been described as uneducated and untrained for her responsibilities. If so, then her on-the-job training was impressive. She was a conscientious queen who fulfilled her public duties despite frequently being in severe pain. She attended more Cabinet meetings in person that any predecessor or successor. She was focused on the finer points of the debates and division within her parliaments.

She sought to be an 'above-party' or at least a 'cross-party' monarch (although her private instincts were Tory, as she was a traditional Anglican and did not want her own powers to be eroded further). She attempted to create ministries and appoint leaders (the concept of a prime minister had not yet developed), who could generate respect and minimise domestic disharmony. It was a noble aim to follow.

It was not fully in tune with the times. It was her misfortune to be queen and search for a non-party approach when the distinctions between Tories and Whigs were becoming more entrenched and the quest for a middle ground in domestic politics more taxing. There were also a series of parliamentary motions of importance where the numbers were close, and defeats led to a rash of general elections.

Anne was compelled to recognise this fragmented politics and, with little appetite, respond to it. She first shifted ground by incorporating a de facto coalition between certain Tories and some Whigs, then conceded authority to the Whigs outright once they had the whip hand in Parliament, and then leaned back towards the Tories (with some relief) when they won election in her last years as Queen.

This was not a balancing act that the monarch would have volunteered for. It was made torture by the breakdown of her relationship with Sarah, Duchess of Marlborough, which took a long time to end.

Originally Sarah Jennings, she had been wed to John Churchill since 1678 and (unlike Anne) had a host of healthy children. She was a woman of strong opinions. She was an unabashed Whig in her politics (almost wearing Anne down by her incessant 'advice' that more Whigs be included in the government) and was of the view that whatever her husband wanted for the War of the Spanish Succession should be provided forthwith, with no quibbling about the expenditure it necessitated.

She also kept diaries. Hundreds and hundreds of pages of them. As her hold on Anne weakened, the tone of what was set out in ink for posterity soured. Anne's unwillingness to heed her counsel was taken as a sign of her ignorance and ingratitude. These volumes are the key source of much of what came after her death to be a dim assessment of Anne as a monarch. This is not an unbiased tome.

It was all made more bitter, considerably more bitter, by the arrival of a new intimate at court who would displace Sarah as the Keeper of the Privy Purse and private confidante within the palace.

Abigail Hill, who after her marriage to a fellow courtier became Abigail Masham, was a cousin of Sarah (she had a host of them, so this did not make them highly familiar to one another), but that branch of the family had fallen on extremely hard times. She would have been seen by some, including the Duchess of Marlborough, as being at the lowly end of the spectrum for a Lady of the Bedchamber. Once it was obvious that she had been utterly usurped in terms of the queen's favour, Sarah marshalled her quill and her voice against her replacement with fervour (including hinting of a lesbian link between them). Whether Anne was wise to be associated with her new best friend can be disputed. She does not seem to have allowed Abigail to promote or prevail against ministerial candidates (unlike Sarah) or seek to shape military doctrine on behalf of her husband. Anne's record should not be judged on it.

She was instead a decent public administrator who did more good than harm. At a minimum, she put her shift in mightily, which is difficult to say of either William III or, particularly later, George I.

Public Opinion

With a fractured political circle, a war that was more of a burden than a blessing, and freakish acts of weather for which the superstitious and the fanatically religious would always look for someone to blame, it would not have been surprising if Anne had often been on the wrong end of public opinion.

She was not. At her ascension she was instantly popular, and despite events she never lost popularity. She started with the advantage that she was not Dutch, was shielded during her reign from the possible charms of the would-be James III because she was clearly not the tool of the French king (at her coronation she had been obliged to make a very long declaration about the dire evils in the doctrine of transubstantiation before she reached the section where the oath was recited), and on her death would be lauded if nothing else because she was not German. None of this was her own doing. If her father had not been quite so careless with the mistress who would become her mother, then it is likely that she would have been the child of a foreign bride and only half-English.

Anne (1702–14)

Her selection of husband, Prince George, turned out to be sound in that the Danes did not create animosity among the English at either the elite or the mass level. He was a reliable Lutheran, but he was willing to take Anglican communion once a year and could exploit the loophole that this allowed for public service, which was nearly but never completely closed by a proposed Occasional Conformity Bill that Anne managed to keep off the statute book. He fancied being (and was) Lord High Admiral. Nobody thought he was the true power behind the throne – in fact, he struggled to fill his daily calendar.

This may have been good fortune, but Anne was aware of it and more than pleased to broadcast it. In her first speech to Parliament, she referred to herself as 'entirely English', and this would be the theme of her reign, that she had an insight into what her subjects thought that others did not have. Her 'small c' conservatism concerning the internal activities and leadership of the Anglican Church also probably suited where the majority of its adherents sat as well, although her desire to stop the Church straying led her to conclude that she should have more control over who were its bishops (a Catholic inclination in other conditions). She established resources to look after impoverished clergy.

She was also more attuned to the economic deprivations of citizens hit by meteorological calamity and the continued corrosive effect of the war than many of those around her. When reports of real hunger among the poor surfaced (as atypically for England they would during this period), she would open up her own stockpiles of food to alleviate it. She saw no disadvantage in letting people be aware of her efforts. It might have been political 'spin', but for an allegedly stupid woman it was a smart means of courting mass favour. She was the last monarch for a long time to meet her end popular.

Financial Competence

As has run continuously through this summary of her reign, the economy was a running sore for Anne. England was innately an extremely rich country, for its merchants at any rate. It was not when trade was badly constrained by conflict, and with exceptional winds and then appalling frosts being seen. There was little means of escape from the cost of conflict without a deft shift in foreign policy (which would come) and none at all from the strange climatic conditions which occurred.

The best that can be said of Anne (and her ministers, who by then were more firmly in the saddle) is that she did not make matters any more difficult than they were destined to be. She can never be accused of personal extravagance – if anything, she was austere. Where she had any flexibility with money, she used it to be a patron of the arts, subsidising George Handel among others. She was interested in aesthetics. No other monarch has a style of furniture named after them in the same way. She did not want war to be funded on a sea of debt, so taxation had to be raised, but with some effort at avoiding the poor paying disproportionately for Marlborough's military miracles. She was wary of irritating the Irish any more than they were already. It was all rather hand-to-mouth, and she was no Henry VII on matters of money. She was no Elizabeth I either. This was a troublesome decade to be in charge.

Foreign Policy

It did not have the scale or the slaughter of the Great War slightly more than 200 years on, but the War of the Spanish Succession was still the defining activity of its era. England (now Britain) had not really been drawn into anything like it since the Hundred Years' War (and that was very much on a stop-start basis). That it came just after William III had pursued the Nine Years' War (1688–97) made the economic, political and social fallout all feel harsher (and his had been a more narrowly confined struggle geographically, involving the Netherlands, England and France). Although casualties in the First World War would be far worse, at least that carnage was contained to only four years in duration.

There had to come an hour when someone appreciated that the War of the Spanish Succession would not be concluded by a total conquest of one side or the other, let alone an unconditional surrender. At the top levels in England, there was disagreement between the Tories (who could be cool about Marlborough regardless of his triumphs, wanted more naval and less land engagement and fretted about the cost of the war) and the Whigs (pro-Marlborough, pro-army and far more anti-French than they were pro-fiscal stability).

Anne was placed uneasily between these factions, increasingly alienated from Marlborough but ill at ease with dispensing of such a hero, agnostic on what armed forces to employ, only hostile to France and its king in so far as they were a menace to her, and concerned about the price of further fighting.

A negotiated outcome was the least bad option. It became Anne's settled position. After far too long spent dodging the bullet, the Duke of Marlborough was dismissed and his wife was finally removed from the queen's sight, retiring to spend more time with her memoirs. A course was being set.

It would be advanced by Henry St John, Viscount Bolingbroke. It took the form of the Treaty of Utrecht of 1713. It was a compromise. It allowed Philip V, the grandson of Louis XIV, to remain King of Spain, but he had to renounce all rights to the throne of France (thus avoiding France swallowing Spain whole, which was what had seized William III in the first place). The strategic ports of Minorca (on what transpired to be a temporary lease) and Gibraltar (up to and including the present day) went to Great Britain. Britain also secured the monopoly rights for thirty years over the transatlantic slave trade, which was seen as a commercial coup back then but does not feature prominently in contemporary UK accounts. It would be hard to contend that this made the War of the Spanish Succession a profitable engagement overall (for anyone, not just England), but it was a respectable pact, and it terminated the war.

It was not without (Whig) critics in Westminster. To smooth its ratification in the House of Lords, the queen had to rig the numbers with twelve new peers, a distasteful but unavoidable ploy. That one of them was the husband of Abigail Masham was not welcomed by her aggrieved cousin.

It was not a beautiful settlement, and it would not prevent yet more strife, but it was a peace with France. It was certainly not all, or mostly, the result of Anne's labours, but it reflected her quiet determination.

Succession

What Anne could not do was produce a healthy child who would live until its maturity and so keep the House of Stuart in business. It can hardly be said that she did not try. Her body, which was not in the best of health over her whole life, was subjected to repeated attempts at pregnancy. It looked like her luck had finally turned with the birth of William, Duke of Gloucester, but he died at 11 in 1700. This must have been a hammer blow and it ushered in the Act of Settlement very shortly afterwards.

She was inclined to think that her fate might have been God's wrath for her treason to her father. She was not as anti-Jacobite as her advisers. In 1696, she had written to the exiled James II to ask for his acceptance of her taking the throne next, while keeping a line open to her half-brother then returning. There are reasons to suspect that she was a sceptic about the Hanoverians, an inclination probably inflamed by the periodic and unconvincing appearance of George, Elector of Hanover, in England. If she privately deduced that the best result would be for the Old Pretender to embrace the Protestant faith (with whatever level of sincerity) and be available as James III, then she would have had a case. Henri IV had, after all, decided that 'Paris was worth a Mass' to be a king. James, alas, was inflexible.

William IV (1830–37)

UNDERRATED

Some have greatness thrust upon them. The word 'greatness' might be overdoing it, but if the standard is the extent to which a monarch exceeds expectations, then William IV is among the top flight of monarchs to sit on the throne. For most of his life, neither he nor more or less anyone thought that he would be King of England, Scotland and Ireland (and Elector of Hanover). He was the third of George III's sons. It was only in the last twenty years of his life, and little more than a dozen years before his elevation actually occurred, that there was any serious prospect that he might be the last man standing and step up when his eldest brother, George IV, fell down. He did not become the heir apparent until after his sixtieth birthday, when the second son, Frederick, Duke of York (the 'Grand Old Duke' of the rhyme), expired in 1827. He became king at the age of 64, the oldest new monarch until Charles III in 2022. Charles, though, had spent a far longer period as the next in line. William did not have many years for his preparation.

It also seemed, at first sight, to be an unfortunate inheritance. George IV was not a loved monarch. His personal extravagance and the manner in which he had sought to dispose of his wife, Caroline of Brunswick, had set the mass public against him and that sentiment would never be reconsidered. His supporters – who were not vast in number, it should be conceded – would argue that first as prince regent and then as king he was a reformed man compared with his early life, which consisted of inappropriate company, huge debts which Parliament had to relieve him of (with little enthusiasm) and an illegal initial marriage. His union with Caroline, a disaster from the moment that he first set eyes on her, had at least (somehow) resulted in Princess Charlotte and the prospect of a direct succession. That option disappeared in 1817 when the death of his daughter rocked the dynasty. It was highly unlikely that George IV would be a father again, and with Frederick also estranged from his other half, William suddenly entered the frame. Even then, with Frederick's wife Princess Frederica Charlotte of Prussia drawing her last breath in 1820, there was the chance that he might marry again and belatedly provide an heir. If this was a contest between the brothers, Frederick was not playing.

As for most of his years William did not consider himself to be a king-in-waiting, he did not behave like one (then again, neither did his eldest brother and he *was* a king-in-waiting). For that reason, he was taken by some to be a fool or, if not that bad, then definitely second-rate material. He acquired the nickname 'Silly Billy'; indeed, many claim it was coined for him. It was not obvious that he would have either the tact or the temperament to handle his responsibilities well, which was a disturbing notion as the combination of class agitation and George IV's massively adverse legacy meant that it was now not inconceivable that radical, republican and even revolutionary ideas might take hold in England.

Turmoil of this sort was being witnessed at this time on the continent, and not merely in France (by now the usual suspect for violent discontent) but in seemingly more stable locations. As it transpired, the fact that William did not have many decades of taking himself too seriously as a presumptive king was an asset. It meant that when he had to make choices between what would turn out to be the past or the future, he, in the end, made the right call and did not align himself unambiguously with the forces of reaction. This might not have been true if his older brother Frederick had lived long enough to become king, or if William and a young Princess Victoria had predeceased George IV, leaving Ernest Augustus, Duke of Cumberland, the fifth son of George III (the fourth, Edward, Duke of Kent, father of Victoria, having died in 1820), to claim the throne. There is little to suggest that he would have been a monarch of any modernity.

There are three aspects to William's life which make him stand out and may explain his later deeds.

The first is that precisely because no one anticipated that he might become king (he was, at best, the spare spare), he was allowed to have something akin to a career. He joined the Royal Navy at the age of 13 in 1778, enlisting as a midshipman. He was, admittedly, an atypical recruit (not many teenagers come aboard a vessel with their private tutor in tow), but he still socialised with a wider rank of individuals than would have been true if he had been the first born. He travelled extensively, including to the American colonies in the midst of the War of Independence (which supposedly led to George Washington backing a proposed plot to kidnap him off the streets and hold him hostage). He spent a large part of the 1780s outside of the United Kingdom. No heir would have done so.

He also appears to have had a flair for command at sea, even if his status was doubtless part of his pathway to promotion. He was a lieutenant by 1785 and the captain of HMS *Pegasus* a year after. He spent much of his time on the waters off the Americas – be that Newfoundland, Nova Scotia or quite a swathe of the West Indies. He certainly saw life with his own eyes and alongside his fellow sailors. In this he has much in common with Prince Charles and Prince Andrew 200 years later.

In 1788, he assumed the command of HMS *Andromeda*, was made a rear admiral in 1789 and moved to the helm of HMS *Valiant* in 1790. He then returned to dry land but retained the itch to switch back to ships for much of the next 25 years. He was appointed an admiral in 1798 but with no vessel in his charge, and he was most irritated that at no stage during the Napoleonic Wars was he allowed to lead a fighting ship in the context of outright warfare. Years later, in 1827, he became Lord High Admiral, a title that had been in hibernation since 1709 (technically it existed, but it was formed of a committee). This was not a happy experience as he was so aggrieved at not having a specific mission that he took a ship out to sea on his own authority and had to bring it back once George IV ordered him to do so.

Despite this eccentric episode, there is no dispute that William viewed the Navy as his occupation as well as his vocation. His image as 'the Sailor King' did him no harm whatsoever. Frederick, his older brother, also spent a considerable amount of his life in the Army, but that was a more conventional line of travel for the younger son of a monarch (and it would not seem that he had much flair for it). As a life experience, William ended up with a role that may have moulded him better for the monarchy.

His complete absence of airs and graces soon manifested itself in a different way from the 1790s. Although only the third son, he and his association with the English Crown were of a standing that he would have found a match among the more minor continental Protestant royalty – or if that did not transpire, an extremely rich young woman or widow would have been convenient, as he was almost rivalling Prince George in the rattling up of debts, to the horror of his innately austere father. One or the other type of marriage would have been normal.

Instead, William engaged in a liaison which, had there been a full-blown tabloid press in those days, would have dominated the headlines for years. He fell for Dorothea Jordon, a well-known actress and singer of sketchy Irish heritage, who had spent some years on the London stage (not the posh end). As a formal marriage was out of the question (George III would have cut him off) and secret wedlock had no real attraction to him (unlike his older brother), he simply cohabited openly with his lover.

Their partnership lasted for twenty years. It involved no fewer than ten illegitimate children (five of each gender), with all but one surviving to be adults, a remarkably good percentage at that time. They would all take the surname FitzClarence so that there was no doubt as to who was their father.

Whatever George III might have thought of this privately, he did not disown William but offered him occupation of Busby House, which was spacious enough for his platoon of offspring and servants. When the relationship was finally terminated in 1811, he provided reasonable financial terms to Dorothea but on the basis that she would not be seen on a stage again. When she broke that rule, the money ceased, and she would die destitute in 1816. He continued to fund his children for the rest of his life, although there would be endless disagreements over whether they had enough (their demands were insatiable). This is a saga which exceeds any modern royal controversy. It also demonstrated again that William was not a predictable man of court but a very atypical figure.

The final feature is that he was very willing to express his opinions in public, whether they suited George III or George IV or not. In 1789, having alighted on a sabbatical from the sea, he wanted to be rendered a duke, which had the advantage of not merely the distinction but a parliamentary grant. His father was extremely cool about the suggestion and sought to tread water on the subject. His son then turned the tables by letting it be heard that if he was not to become a duke (and so enter the House of Lords), he was minded to put his name forward at the next election to the House of Commons for the Totnes seat (implicitly as a Whig candidate, not the king's preferred Tories).

Measuring Monarchy

This would have caused fireworks. George III decided to cut his losses and elevate William to be Duke of Clarence and St Andrews. He knew full well that this would not proscribe his son from politics.

The duke did avail himself of the benches of the House of Lords and periodically broadcasted there. Although he was mostly in accord with the Whigs, there were some embarrassing deviations. There were gasps when he spoke against the early attempt to abolish slavery within Great Britain itself (the struggle to eliminate it from the entirety of the empire would take a considerable time longer), and he compounded the offence by suggesting that William Wilberforce was a fanatic and that his own time at sea had taught him that slaves in the West Indies had a better deal than free servants in Scotland (an assertion which managed to offend almost everyone). A stretch of strategic silence duly followed.

William would not abandon the public pulpit altogether but plainly mellowed with age (or adjusted his views so that they did not create a hurdle to reaching the throne). He spoke vigorously in favour of Catholic emancipation, triggering a sharp disagreement in the Lords with Ernest Augustus, his younger brother and Duke of Cumberland, who evidently deemed the idea to be appalling (George IV was probably in the same camp but would not put his head above this parapet or many others).

All of this was little short of sensational. It is no wonder that the powers that be were far from sure what would come to pass if and when William took the throne from his reviled brother. Most feared the worst. Many would have been totally nonplussed about the new king. Few started as optimists.

Those few (and it really would not have been an extensive band) were largely to be vindicated. On most of the measures of monarchical success, but with the odd wobble, William IV came through.

William IV (1830–37)

Professional Standing

To the amazement of many, William IV threw himself into the administrative side of the monarchy with some intensity. Paperwork had been piling up as George IV's health had deteriorated (and he did not have much zeal for this part of his post even when he was in better condition). William, it is reported, had been practising his new royal initials in advance and was signing with aplomb. His courtiers and prime ministers (authority having shifted from Palace to Parliament) appreciated this.

William's real tests would be threefold: how he would approach the mooted Great Reform Bill, which the aristocracy naturally assumed that he would want to subvert as dangerous legislation; whether he would accept that the choice of prime minister was not his personal whim but contingent on the will of the House of Commons; and how he might regard a raft of relatively radical legislation, much of which the House of Lords did not care for, but which those of a liberal disposition were convinced was essential to appease mass opinion and so avoid bloody strife.

The test case was the Great Reform Bill. The title of the measure rather overstated its provisions. It sought to deal with a constituency boundary structure that had remained untouched for centuries and which had the surreal effect of ignoring the rise of the likes of Birmingham and Manchester. It had left in place notorious 'rotten boroughs' such as Old Sarum (a total electorate of seven). It would widen the franchise but from a very, very, very small percentage of the population to a very, very small percentage of the population. The statute equivalent of the French Revolution, it was not. For many in the high nobility, with seats in the House of Lords, it was still the thin end of the wedge.

It was thus thin ice for the new monarch. The crisis started in 1831 when Lord Grey's Great Reform Bill was blocked inside

Parliament. This was despite his allies having secured most seats at a hotly contested general election (in so far as a campaign and count with so few voters could properly be dubbed 'hotly contested') in 1830. The notion of a 'mandate' was weak then but not negligible. Grey wanted to return matters to the country for fresh legitimacy and requested a dissolution of Parliament.

It would not have been an outrage if William had turned him down. There had been an election only a year earlier. The king mulled over the request but was edging towards granting Grey his hustings. To shut that down, a sizeable section of the House of Lords started to agitate for the fast passage of an address which would specifically forbid the dissolution of Parliament without the Lords' blessing.

This was a red rag to a bull for William. It was a usurpation of his (and only his) prerogative powers. It was also an assault on the unwritten constitution, in that it indicated that a totally unelected Lords could veto the preference for consulting the voters of the (quite substantially unelected) Commons. Brushing aside the claim that logistical difficulties prevented him from traversing to Westminster, William charged towards the House of Lords, donned a crown and personally dissolved Parliament. When the (tiny) numbers of votes were cast in the election, the reformers swept the board.

This did not mean plain sailing. The Commons were in favour of the bill, but the Lords threw it out. Grey asked the king to state that he would create a new wave of peers to pass the legislation. The king was not wild about this scheme but wanted to resolve the impasse. The Lords backed down but switched to killing off the legislation by countless destructive amendments. Grey came back with the demand for more peers. William then made his only mistake: he accepted Grey's resignation and signalled to the Duke of Wellington that he might seek to form another government. The latter did not have the numbers and it was obvious that the public would not stomach him as prime minister. William reversed his stance at considerable speed, reinstated Grey and with gritted teeth let the Upper House know that if they pushed him again, he would swamp their chamber with new peers. Once that was unmistakable, the Lords threw in the towel and by their abstention the bill became law.

This was an almighty political dispute with an importance which went well beyond the brutal truth that the Representation of the People Act of 1832 had expanded the electorate from 400,000 to about 650,000 or around 20 per cent of adult males (there was some double counting, so the actual proportion would be slightly lower). In many ways this was an even more incremental and conservative change than it appeared, as it explicitly deprived the few women who had the vote of that prize. Meanwhile, the separate Scottish Reform Act boosted the number with the franchise by more than twelvefold, albeit from a low base of approximately 5,000 individuals. The line in the sand, nonetheless, was about the balance of power between the House of Commons and the House of Lords and William had sided with the Commons.

None of this directly altered William's own constitutional authority. The second test came when Grey wanted to stand down as prime minister and allow Viscount Melbourne to succeed him. This was not a seismic move in itself, but Melbourne insisted that Lord John Russell be the leader in the Commons (confusingly, one could be a lord in the Commons if you were not the primary family title holder). William had no time for Lord Russell and thought him an agitator. He effectively sacked Melbourne and asked Sir Robert Peel to form an administration. Peel could not command a majority in the House of Commons, so an election was held in which the Conservatives again lost to the Liberals.

Having fallen short at the ballot box, as it were (they did not exist in British elections then), the king relented in an amicable spirit, recalled Melbourne to be prime minister and put up with

Lord John Russell occupying the most senior slot in the House of Commons. It was done with sufficient grace to limit the damage. It could have been a much more brutal political battle. William had accepted the principle that his choice of prime minister was dependent on the will of a majority in the Commons. In so doing, the keystone of the constitutional monarchy arch had been laid and it would stay. The professional standing of the king would be enhanced even as his personal authority waned.

The final uncertainty was whether the monarch might, overtly or covertly, attempt to impede a conveyor belt of other transformative legislation that the House of Lords invariably disliked. He did not. In short order, the Factory Act (1833), the Slavery Act (1833), the Poor Law Amendment Act (1834) and other liberalising measures in England and remedial initiatives in Ireland were adopted. What William considered of them privately is guesswork, but his signature for Royal Assent was reliable. He emerges from all of these episodes as a proper professional when it came to his official obligations.

Public Opinion

With the exception of the short moment during the trials and tribulations of the Great Reform Bill when he did not back Grey to the hilt, all the evidence is that William IV was consistently popular.

Not being George IV was an extremely solid start. He was the polar opposite. He was very pleased to be king and wanted others – the poor as well as the rich – to be pleased that he was king as well. On the first day of his reign, he was spotted hurtling through the capital in a carriage, doffing his hat, smiling and waving at all and sundry, accepting kisses from strangers and even offering passers-by a ride. This was not the normal approach of the House of Hanover, which was stiff, not touchy-feely. The evidence is that it was completely sincere. William had come to the throne unexpectedly and late in life and was inclined to ensure that everyone including himself enjoyed the experience.

This was not an affectation either. In the course of his reign, he would often walk unaccompanied in both London and Brighton and strike up conversations with those around him. He was a free spirit. He could also be a little shameless in his ambition to win over hearts and minds. He dispensed of the French chefs and the German bands which his brother had relied on and replaced them with English alternatives. He ostentatiously paid little attention to his additional post as Elector of Hanover, other than agreeing to a new constitution which embraced middle-class aspirations (his starkly different brother Ernest Augustus would terminate that trend as soon as he replaced William IV in Hanover). He was the most English (and the least pretentious) of the Hanoverian kings, which went down well. He had many traits which we would now connect to the 'bicycling monarchs' of the Netherlands or the Nordic countries, and as such is the personal repudiation of the thesis that this more relaxed style has no history in Britain. For William, popularity had a purpose; it did not devalue him to press the flesh in person.

Financial Competence

The more than 125 years between the end of William III's reign and the start of William IV's tenure had seen the monarchy cease to be held responsible for the financial affairs of the nation. There was now a Treasury and a Bank of England, and the structure of the public finances, such as they were, had shifted from parliamentary assent to parliamentary oversight. This may have been a mutual relief, given the contorted financial difficulties which many of those who preceded William had landed themselves in, with hard repercussions for ordinary people. The king's head remained on the coinage, but it was no longer a silver coinage for him to debase if he wanted to.

This makes comparisons about financial competence across time an uninspiring use of valuable time. A better lens to look at the later monarchs such as William IV is how they handled their own material affairs, as much of what they did would necessitate substantial subsidy from overall taxation.

Once more, if George IV was yin, then William IV was yang. It was not so much that he was parsimonious as that he did not see the reason for expenditure for the sake of it. His ego did not need to be sated by big spending.

There were three highly visible illustrations of this new attitude to public money. The first involved his coronation. William took some convincing that he needed to hold one at all, as the absence of the ceremony had not prevented him from placing a crown on his head when entering into the House of Lords during the Great Reform Bill uproar. Once it was accepted that a coronation was compulsory, William wanted the cut-price option on the menu. His brother had secured a grant of £240,000 to fund his coronation (an event best remembered for the loud howls of the crowd against the king as Caroline of Brunswick made a doomed effort to enter the ceremony). William spent under £30,000. It was such a modest affair that traditionalists complained Britain had become a 'half-crown' nation.

The second stand taken was on Buckingham Palace. George IV had lavished a fortune on the site. His younger brother made it known that he disapproved of the expenditure and refused outright to live there. He even conspired to hand it over to another institution of the state, first as an army barracks and later to Parliament after the 1834 fire which had destroyed its existing site. Paradoxically, it was Parliament that actually preferred a brand-new, grand location for itself, not a second-hand home.

Finally, William, who was no patron of the arts, handed most of George IV's paintings to the nation. This would open them up to a much wider community and serve the cultural interest far better.

Foreign Policy

Much as with the country's finances, direct control over foreign policy was not in the hands of the monarch exclusively, but a king could have opinions and exercise a sophisticated influence.

His short reign meant that William IV could do little more than touch the foreign policy tiller. He had views and he could be far-sighted. He remained deeply wary of the French (this was an age in which that country moved between different constitutional models at alarming pace) and made no effort in that direction. He was more intrigued by the United States, possibly because of his time there as a young sailor, and lavished flattery on that country and the American ambassador in London, singling out George Washington for wholesome praise (he was probably unaware of the very first president's readiness to allow others to kidnap the youthful Prince William), and this was noticed in America. He could see the tantalising possibilities of the proposed Suez Canal and the desirability of cultivating Egypt so that it would be constructed in a way that met British interests. He was vocal in favouring Belgian independence, which might seem an obscure subject now but was not then. He was cautious about the merits of war, but his seven years were in any case calm in terms of conflict. He had sound judgement but also understood that he was not a commander-in-chief without chains.

Succession

The one metric on which William IV did not cross the bar was succession, in that he did not leave a child of his own who was qualified to replace him. Had he known earlier in his life that he would be king, then he surely would have met that test as his ten children out of wedlock with his partner suggest that, in his prime, he would have made up for the singularly poor output of his brothers. When he did appreciate that he might be placed on the throne, he went in search of a bride who would end the drought of sons and daughters of the sons of George III. He was wed to Adelaide of Saxe-Meiningen, who had several unsuccessful pregnancies, only one of which resulted in a baby (Princess Elizabeth) who made it beyond a couple of months of age before dying. If she had not expired, then there would have been a Queen Elizabeth II in 1837, not one who ascended to the throne some 115 years afterwards.

William was fond of and wanted to be close to his niece and heir, Princess Victoria. Her mother, the widow of brother Edward, the Duchess of Kent and Strathearn, was irrationally hostile towards him. She would not let her daughter near his court, which would impede her constitutional education. At what would be his last birthday banquet in August 1836, William lashed out at his foe and told those there that it was his fervent wish to survive until Victoria reached the age of 18, so that her mother would never be regent. He managed that with a month to spare. Even in death he exceeded expectations.

Victoria (1837–1901)

OVERRATED

Causality or coincidence? That is the fundamental question which should be asked in the assessment of Queen Victoria. She is frequently mentioned as among the most significant of British monarchs, but it is not entirely clear why. All too often it is because the Victorian era, especially its 'golden age' in economic terms (1850–70) and territorial expansion (1880–1900), which are rightly recalled as representing close to the zenith of national influence and power, are conflated with the queen herself, as if the latter was in some sense, any sense frankly, directly responsible for the former.

This is a supposition which is absurd. So, it is softened by devices such as claiming that Victoria should be credited with 'presiding over' these glory days (which she did not), or at a less demanding level, 'symbolising' the might of Great Britain at the height of its dominance of the world order (which may be true but did not require much in the way of heavy lifting for the monarch herself), or at an absolute minimum, doing nothing from the throne which obstructed the rise and rise of *Pax*

Britannica (yet even this, very tepid endorsement is capable of some dissection).

To put this in context, the country had already changed sufficiently that by 1837 the king or queen had ceased to be the de facto chief executive of Great Britain PLC and was instead rather closer to a non-executive chair (en route to the post of honorary life president), so it could be countered that it is unreasonable to expect that Victoria might be the driving force for the age in which she lived and reigned. This is undoubtedly true and was acknowledged by her contemporaries. As early as 1867, Walter Bagehot, the towering constitutional thinker and writer of his time, asserted that a monarch now had only the right to be consulted, to encourage and to warn. A different king or queen from Victoria might, nonetheless, have been a more important actor than she turned out to be. The fall in the monarch's authority over politics between William IV and Victoria is striking, even though his tenure was little more than a tenth in duration of hers. Others to come later had more impact.

To put the matter differently, perhaps indelicately, let us conduct a thought experiment. Suppose that Princess Charlotte of Wales, who died in childbirth in 1817 at the age of 21, had been looked after far better in the hours that followed the delivery of her stillborn son, and had survived the experience. Suppose that she lived to succeed her father in 1830 at still a comparatively youthful age and reigned for much of the rest of the century (still to be there in 1900 she would have had to hit 104, but put that to one side). Is there good reason to think that the 'Charlotte era' would have been markedly distinct from the Victorian one? In a reflection of how these matters functioned then, the husband of Princess Charlotte was Prince Leopold of Saxe-Coburg-Saalfeld, later the inaugural King of Belgium. After Charlotte's death, Edward, Duke of Kent, Victoria's father, would wed Leopold's sister.

Victoria (1837–1901)

From an alternative angle, imagine that Charlotte's son had not been stillborn but had breathed from the very first, even if his mother had still sadly died largely due to medical neglect, and that he had assumed the throne after his grandfather (presumably as George V) in 1830 and sat on it until 1900, reaching a more plausible 83 years of age by then. Would we conclude that Britain might not have been the workshop of the world or acquired an empire on which the sun never set?

Finally, among this set of not incredible 'what ifs?', allow that William, then Duke of Clarence, had seen the daughter, Princess Elizabeth, born to him and his wife in 1820, be of a very robust well-being and that she, not Victoria, had acquired the Crown in 1837, and lived to see the new century in, at the age of 80. Are there persuasive grounds for concluding that an 'Elizabethan era' would never been witnessed?

If the answers to all these questions, counterfactual as they as, are 'no', then the thesis that Victoria and the Victorian era are interchangeable and interconnected manifestly lacks credibility. In that case, the correct approach is to assess Victoria on the same five metrics as the rest of this volume. While an analysis of this kind is far from damning, it also makes an 'overrated' grade irresistible.

To take this line of assertion further, we could look to more contemporary examples. If someone were to mount a defence of General Franco on the basis that Real Madrid dominated European football in the late 1950s, this would be considered ludicrous. If it were articulated that, as Harold Wilson was the British prime minister (1964–70) at almost exactly the same period as The Beatles became the biggest musical phenomenon in the world, he and not the many other claimants should be considered 'the fifth Beatle', such words would rightly be considered ridiculous ('All You Need Is Love' never replaced 'The Red Flag' as the Labour Party anthem in the 1960s). If an admirer of Richard Nixon were to swear that his presence in the Oval

Office when the first man landed on the moon mattered more than the inept cover-up of the Watergate burglary mounted at the same site, the proponent of that proposition would, entirely correctly, be slated as preposterous (the N in NASA never stood for Nixon). It would be, to borrow from a film title, the *Being There* outlook on history.

The starting point for an analysis of Victoria as queen should be the features of the so-called Victorian era and whether there is anything there that should be ascribed to her personally.

To summarise extremely succinctly, there are five strands of the Victorian era worth highlighting.

The first is that, in stark contrast to what was witnessed elsewhere, Britain made a measured and phased transition towards being a parliamentary democracy based on popular sovereignty. This was hardly rushed, but it was a more comprehensive exercise than was undertaken in most of Europe and secured the country a reputation for political stability that until recently continued to be accepted.

It had begun with the Great Reform Act of 1832, which William IV had seen through Parliament. It would be augmented by a Second Reform Act of 1867 (masterminded by Benjamin Disraeli at the helm of a minority administration), then supplemented by the Ballot Act of 1872, which installed secret voting and the 'Australian ballot' in place of the obviously suspect showing of hands as the means by which the electorate translated its wishes into the selection of Members of Parliament. It would be topped up by a Third Reform Act in 1884, this time the output of William Gladstone. While it could be said that the country was behind the curve in the speed at which it implemented change, the balance struck was strong enough that the Chartist movement never threatened the old order.

What this left by 1900 was hardly a full democracy. A bare majority of men might have satisfied the qualifications needed to vote, but women were still disenfranchised. There were British colonies – Australia, Canada and New Zealand – which were more progressive. By European norms, Great Britain was, nonetheless, enlightened. The cry in the First World War that the UK was on the democratic side in opposition to the autocracies of Germany and Austro-Hungary was not a laughable piece of rhetoric.

Is there any reason, to raid Bagehot's formulation, that this was a course of action which the queen had exercised her right 'to encourage'? None whatsoever. At best she was indifferent to the moves and at worst she thought them risky, particularly any legislation that Mr Gladstone put forward.

An important second aspect of the Victorian era is the manufacturing might of Great Britain. The Industrial Revolution had been born in England in the eighteenth century but went, literally, full steam ahead in the century thereafter. The initial innovations were advanced further by the coming of the railways. Other improvements in transportation would follow. They were allied by an astonishing revolution in communications courtesy of the telegram, the telephone and, towards the very end, an early radio.

While the rewards for all this were not distributed evenly, real wages went upwards. This was not a linear trend: the British economy was at its strongest from 1820 to 1873, stagnated in many respects from 1873 to 1896 and then recovered some momentum. Part of the decline in the middle was that Britain was facing unwelcome competition from Germany and the United States for its markets. Angst about this was sizeable and led to a Royal Commission on the Depression in Trade and Industry (1885–86), which had to steer its way between a disagreement between traditional free traders (predominantly Liberals) and an emerging lobby for 'fair trade' (largely Conservatives). This would be a dispute that dominated economic debate in the thirty years after Victoria had expired.

Was the queen any part of this course of events or the deliberations about what to do in the 1880s? Plainly not. Prince Albert might merit an honourable mention for taking an interest, and for his role in the Great Exhibition of 1851, which after a rocky start came to be seen as a huge success, but in all other respects the Victorian era and Victoria herself are like ships passing each other in the night.

The third realm was science, where Great Britain thought of itself as a hothouse. This was an age of discovery, although some of what emerged, notably Charles Darwin and his theory of evolution, was the cause of controversy and contention. The nation did not serve as the overlord of science to the extent that it liked to think (the universities were not the incubators of ideas that they were to become in the twentieth century), but there was more than enough that was seen as new and exciting, including the benefits of electricity, to captivate those who were intrigued by science. Once again, Victoria was a non-playing captain in this sector. Her husband was perhaps a twelfth man.

The fourth (and last domestic) category encompasses social reform and cultural enrichment. In a less than coordinated way, slum clearance and a concentration on public health acquired a standing. Compulsory education was introduced. There was the mass circulation of literature (not only that of Charles Dickens), and popular music and sport became forms of entertainment for many people. The concept of travel, whether within Britain or further afield, obtained a vogue (with Thomas Cook in the lead). There was a tension between the opportunity for enjoyment and the moral strictures of many within the Victorian elite (the queen belonged in the second camp; her eldest son and heir, the first). It all made for a very different country. The monarch herself had little if anything to do with this.

Finally, and in many ways more memorably, there was imperialism. This was not universally approved of. The Conservatives, having once been 'Little Englanders', saw the empire as both a good in itself and a means by which to appeal to an expanding electorate, to which they might otherwise have little to offer.

The Liberals were more convinced internationalists but felt that empire had to have an ethical purpose if the expenditure of money and men in its pursuit was to be legitimate. Having spent the better part of 1,000 years being obsessed by France, the new Great Britain raised its sights to a much wider world, and a hallmark of the Victorian era is the confidence with which it came to do so. The queen was rewarded with the title of Empress of India and seems to have taken a keen interest in the affairs of the subcontinent. She also followed the twists and turns of the 'scramble for Africa' with, in her final days, very firm and unflattering views about the Boers, who had become an enemy.

By this part of her reign, though, which is different from her earlier attempts to shape foreign policy that will be outlined later, Victoria was a cheerleader. That so much of the world had come to be painted pink on a map by 1900 was a process in which she and the monarchy were, in candour, bystanders.

Victoria and the Victorian era have to be seen separately. One was not the mother to the other. It would be immensely charitable to rank Victoria among the highest stratum of monarchs just because she managed to be alive at the right time, acquire the throne when young and live an unusually long life. Her conduct and her record have to be assessed on the same five yardsticks used for the others.

Professional Standing

Victoria's reputation among those who knew her well and worked with her is, to be kind, patchy. It did not help that a malicious mother had not allowed William IV to school her as he wished, had tried to make her own confidant and probable lover, Sir John Conroy, the *éminence grise* to the new queen (Victoria froze him out) and had insisted on living in Buckingham Palace until her daughter had married. Inexperience was certainly an element in the misjudgements which brought Victoria's judgement into doubt.

Some of her major miscalculations lasted for the entire length of her reign, so inexperience is not an alibi. Her professionalism was consistently undermined by her personal views about politicians. She had favourites (it was obvious who they were) and she had hate figures (who knew who they were). A constitutional monarch, as William IV understood better if not perfectly, had to rise above all this.

Her preferences affected public administration. She was far too close to Lord Melbourne, her first prime minister (so much so that she was soon referred to as 'Mrs Melbourne' by detractors). He may have been the father figure that she never had (her own had died before her first birthday). It came across as partisanship. It was the source of embarrassment when in 1839, Melbourne, having been defeated in a vote in the House of Commons, sought to resign as prime minister. Shocked, the queen had to approach Sir Robert Peel, a Tory, to construct an administration. As was accepted form then, he insisted that all the existing Ladies of the Bedchamber (an unofficial source of advice to the queen), who were then collectively associated with the Whigs/Liberals, should be replaced by a collection of a more Conservative disposition. Ignoring precedent, Victoria refused his instruction. Peel declined to take office. Melbourne had to be brought back for two more years as premier. At the election of 1841, Peel and the Conservatives won handsomely. The queen was left looking foolish.

This was a pattern which would be repeated consistently. Having acquired Peel, Victoria (and Albert) took a shine to him. The prime minister would fall after the repeal of the Corn Laws, a critical move to meet the massive crisis that the Great Famine had created in Ireland. The royal couple then clashed on a regular basis with Lord Palmerston, first when he was foreign secretary and again when he became prime minister. She was unmistakably taken by Benjamin Disraeli who, as he conceded, laid on the flattery 'with a trowel', but she could even have hissy fits with him, threatening several times that she would abdicate while pressing her prime minister to be far more hawkish against Russia in the Russo-Turkish War of the 1870s (Disraeli would, however, achieve what he wanted at the Congress of Berlin). This was all straying far beyond the Bagehot tripod of being consulted, encouraging or warning.

This was but a warm-up act to her relationship, if that is the proper term, with William Gladstone. When the Liberals won the 1880 election with Gladstone (notionally a backbench MP but plainly at the centre of the campaign), she first sought a means of blocking his appointment, with the unsubtle hint of abdication again in the air, before finally bowing to the unavoidable. Such was her open venom for him that, with Disraeli now dead and the Marquis of Salisbury yet to complete his rise, she might as well have applied for the post of Leader of the Opposition. Her contempt for her prime minister was not an open secret; it was no secret. She would twist the knife with incidents such as sending an uncoded telegram to Gladstone at his home address chastising him for the death of General Gordon at Khartoum in 1883, with the high probability, which was duly realised, that the railway station master would read the missive and so her admonishment would be publicly known.

While some on the very outside of her circle, including the Prince of Wales, tried to smooth these controversies over, she did not relent. When Gladstone became prime minister for the fourth and final time in 1892, she vetoed one of his choices for the Cabinet and continued to attack him. By now it might have been better for all concerned if their dialogue had been conducted through lawyers.

The one period of her reign when in a sense she did not interfere in parliamentary politics came with the death of Prince Albert in late 1861. Albert had long been her chief adviser.

He was more flexible than her and less disposed to take an instant loathing to certain people, but he also had some bees in his bonnet. It stretched the constitution to have the queen behave as she often did, as the notion of her husband being anything akin to a second pair of eyes on official paperwork was completely out of order (as Prince George of Denmark, the hapless husband of Queen Anne, who found himself with nothing to occupy his time with, could have ruefully testified).

Interference, however, was in many ways better than invisibility. With the loss of her beloved Albert (for which on some contorted reasoning her eldest son and heir was blamed), the queen entered her 'Widow of Windsor' internal exile amid a mountain of mourning. She withdrew to Windsor Castle and after that spent a substantial amount of time at Balmoral (in the company of a manservant, John Brown, which set many a tongue wagging back in London). She refused to open Parliament and was barely seen in public. If a glimpse was caught of her, then she would be dressed in black and make no attempt at personal engagement. It was like the madness of King George (III), except that she was not insane and the option of nominating a regent in her place was unavailable.

It would be incorrect to suggest that Victoria was an absentee monarch entirely. Correspondence was sent to her, and it would, in her time, be dealt with. As far as the wider public was aware, she was on strike (albeit out of grief, not aiming for gratification) rather than, as might be more accurate, in an emotional state where she only felt capable of working to rule. Government did not grind to a halt in this time, but it was a dislocation to the system, and no one could tell when, if at all, it might end. It was a subject which was totally impossible to raise with the woman herself. It was a state of stasis.

This was not an ideal time for the monarchy to seem to have abandoned its responsibilities. Victoria's disappearance from London life was a matter of continuous discussion, but that she was not there did not prevent another Reform Act being adopted, or curtail industry, sabotage scientific advance, stop the rise of association football or other pastimes, or cause the empire to shrink. Britain was functioning with a mothballed monarchy and did not seem adversely affected by the situation.

That might tempt some people, institutions and organisations to ask aloud whether the country truly needed not only this queen but any head of state of this form. There was a fresh example of an alternative to be found in France where, after the Prussian victory in 1871, the old regime had gone, and a Third Republic had emerged into the sunlight. Over the decades it would prove to be a chronic system of government (although it endured until another invasion from the east did for it in 1940), but at its birth it was rather more enticing. Republicanism started to become a respectable position. Sir Charles Dilke, a prominent Liberal, was the first politician of sound Establishment credentials to break rank and publicly ponder whether the monarchy should be scrapped for a republic. Others were less direct than him but were willing to speculate about whether the institution was worth the money spent to maintain it. Before the die was cast, without fanfare, Victoria came back into the limelight. All was forgiven, not forgotten. That was often the rule when it came to her contested professional standing.

Public Opinion

Public opinion regarding the queen had a yo-yo quality to it. This was partly because the coverage of the monarchy was now more extensive as magazines sought to attract readers. Society was also not as deferential as it had been. Bagehot's plea for self-restraint from the throne ('not let in daylight on magic'[9]) was

---

9   Walter Bagehot, *The English Constitution* (1867).

behind the times. The royals could not expect to serve behind a screen of silence.

To start with there was a great deal of goodwill towards the young new monarch. Some of this was lost in the bizarre story of the affair of Lady Flora Hastings. The woman concerned had a swelling in a place which suggested pregnancy and was thought to have been the subject of Sir John Conroy's amorous advances. Victoria, who by now was completely at odds with Sir John, decided that the rumours were well founded and expelled Lady Flora from civilised society. It turned out that the poor woman was the victim of a vast cancerous tumour and would die soon after it was established.

The queen's poll ratings (if they could have been conducted then) suffered another blow with her marriage to Prince Albert. He was labelled by some as a 'pauper prince' and so a gold-digger. There was a tussle over the allowance that Parliament would agree to offer him. It was evident that he did not hold the opinion that he should be neither seen nor heard, and acted instead as a co-monarch. This further disturbed Victoria's already tense dealings with prime ministers and parliaments. It was not until 1857 that Lord Palmerston (despite Victoria's sniping at him) had him made prince consort.

Her popularity soared after an ineffective assassination attempt in 1840 (the would-be murderer, Edward Oxford, had a clear view to fire his gun, but failed to take his chance). Assailants would also try and fail to eliminate her again in 1842 (twice), 1849, 1850, 1871 and 1882. Every shot missed made her more appreciated by the public. Her status, having declined during her 'Widow of Windsor' phase, rose when she re-emerged from mourning and soared during her Golden Jubilee of 1887 and her Diamond Jubilee ten years later. By then she had been rebranded as grandmother of the nation.

Financial Competence

Even more so than under William IV, the monarchy had ceased to be the leader in this area. The only point of comment at the time and subsequently is how the queen handled her (taxpayer) resources. While not as careful as her uncle had been, apart from when she had isolated herself at Windsor and Balmoral and was seen (wrongly) to be doing nothing, she was not an extravagant figure with money. She was cautious, even frugal; she had no desire to dress to impress or erect an array of palaces.

Foreign Policy

She had more interest in foreign affairs and often sought to push ministers towards her preferences. Albert was an activist in this area as well. He may have instigated her enquiries. She was content to be an instrument in a rapprochement with France in the 1840s and 1850s. She was at odds with Lord Palmerston, who wanted to exploit the political earthquakes of 1848 in continental Europe to divide and rule, whereas Victoria favoured full-on support for the monarchies under siege. While much of the country swooned when the smooth Italian radical Giuseppe Garibaldi visited in 1864, the queen (although secluded in Windsor anyway) did not share the sentiment. She would never have met him.

There would be further disharmony with Lord Palmerston. In the earliest stages of the Crimea crisis, Victoria and Albert were doves, preferring to avoid war, whereas the foreign secretary was firmly pro-Turkish and anti-Russian. The public were with Palmerston and the royal duo then relented. In the first weeks of the American Civil War, Palmerston tacitly backed the southern secession (as it would damage the United States, an economic rival, through division), whereas Albert was more ambivalent.

A set of miscalculations after the prince consort's death almost saw Great Britain and the forces led by Abraham Lincoln come to blows. While ensconced in Windsor, the Prusso-Danish War blew up. The government, notably Lord John Russell, favoured Copenhagen. The monarch inclined to Berlin.

With Albert out of the way, once she resumed her duties in full, Victoria became less immersed in the detail of foreign relations. Europe was less interesting than India and the extension of empire. She was more than willing to lend her name to the blueprint which Disraeli and after him Lord Salisbury had constructed. Yet this was – and hardly for the first time as she was a repeat offender – a partisan position. Disraeli's amoral but effective pragmatism in European politics offended many. In the 1870s he played all sides off against each other, while Gladstone, at his most sermonising best, took issue with the 'Balkan Atrocities' and was more sceptical about the rush to acquire colonies in Africa at all costs in the last two decades of the nineteenth century. Victoria's forays in foreign policy invariably had little impact (and for the first twenty-five years of her tenure can be ascribed to Prince Albert to a major extent). The question is not if she was right but whether she should have stayed out of it. As with her professional standing overall, she did not have a strong grasp of constitutional monarchy.

Succession

In one sphere, providing for the succession, it must be conceded that Victoria did her bit. Had she been shot dead in 1840, then her uncle Ernest Augustus, King of Hanover, would have been the next in line, which would have endangered the monarchy as an entity, such was his unpopularity. The risk of that soon disappeared as Victoria produced nine children in eighteen years and proceeded to marry them off to the royalty of Europe, a bond that became troublesome come the Great War. She had a very difficult relationship with the Prince of Wales, her eldest son and heir, but that is hardly unique in British history. Even Mr Gladstone would have commended her on succession planning.

Victoria is as much a myth as a monarch. As queen she was highly flawed. She was linked to an age in which Great Britain flourished. She was not a catalyst for this. She is a highly overrated figure.

Edward VII (1901–10)

UNDERRATED

There is a tendency to assume that long reigns are a necessary (but not sufficient) condition for successful reigns. Although there are some obvious exceptions, including Henry III (1216–72), Henry VI (1422–61 and 1470–71) and George III (1760–1820), the assumption is understandable. Surely a monarch requires a decent stretch of time to make any kind of impact. In the case of Edward VII, by contrast, although it is unfortunate that he did not live long enough to have the chance of exercising some sway in the final years before the outbreak of the First World War, he did more than enough during nine years on the throne to be considered a figure of real stature and an energetic innovator. He has been treated as if a sort of bookend to the lengthy reign of his mother, Victoria. He was more than that.

It is remarkable, allowing for his upbringing, that Edward was in a psychological state to achieve anything. The second child of Queen Victoria, from birth he was subject to his father's almost pathological idea of what the ideal education and training for a constitutional monarch should be and his mother's lack of obvious affection for him (although, as she spent much of his formative years pregnant with his many siblings, her distraction is perhaps understandable). Both parents all but gave up on him well before he compounded the divide by all too obviously relishing pleasure. He was dismissed as stupid and lacking in the character that Victoria's take on what a monarch should be demanded. The fear, and it was at times explicit, was that he would be the reincarnation of George IV, an experience that no one who wanted to see monarchy survive would have wished repeated.

This indifference continued into his adult life. Victoria seems to have persuaded herself that it was the revelation that the Prince of Wales had spent three nights in a sexual liaison with an actress that compelled an outraged Prince Albert to travel to shame him, despite being unwell, after which he fully contracted the typhoid fever from which he subsequently expired. For a decade he was very close to being a *persona non grata* in her company and household, and he only experienced an improvement in their relationship when, a decade after his father, he too was hit by typhoid fever and nearly died.

Even this would not be the cause of a complete reconciliation. Victoria denied him access to state papers (others, notably William Gladstone as prime minister, found means of smuggling them to him), his frequent offers to engage in diplomacy on her behalf, particularly while she was the Widow of Windsor, were usually rejected and she did not allow him to act as her deputy until 1898.

Victoria and Albert not only misunderstood their own child (a forgivable error) but also failed to see that while there was one member of the House of Hanover whom the then Prince of Wales, later King Edward VII, resembled, it was not George IV but his successor, the altogether distinctive William IV.

The comparison is not perfect, but it has value to it. Both came to the throne late in life, William IV when 64, Edward VII at 59. The difference, of course, was that for most of his life

Edward VII (1901–10)

William IV did not think that he was likely to be king, whereas from his earliest sentient experiences Edward was all too aware of the burden that would be placed on his shoulders. He was constantly reminded of his duty. When they finally ascended to the throne, both William IV and Edward VII would make the most of it.

William had created a career for himself in the Navy. Edward wanted to do something similar but in the Army. Victoria vetoed that idea as unsuitable for the heir to the Crown. He was allowed to spend some time with the armed forces, but it was limited and safe in its situation. No risks were taken.

Both men travelled far more extensively than their royal relatives had been willing to do. The young Edward went on a tour of the United States and Canada in 1860, on the eve, as it turned out, of the American Civil War, which would have made such a trip impossible in the next five years. He attracted an enormous amount of positive attention and stayed with President James Buchanan at The President's Mansion (a building which in 1814 British troops had tried to raze to the ground; it had to be repainted white to cover the scorch marks). He attended a service at Trinity Church in New York City, during which prayers were offered for the health of the British royal family for the first time in the United States since 1776. The prince, far from being the duffer that his parents had decided he was, had star quality.

It would not be the only example of him going longer-haul. In 1862, he went on an extensive visit to the Middle East, incorporating Egypt, Jerusalem, Damascus, Istanbul and Beirut, with the ulterior motive for ministers of outsmarting the French in this region while the Suez Canal was under construction. Whether the queen's willingness to let him undertake this assignment was a rare instance of warmth towards him or because in the months after the death of Albert she could not stand the sight of her son is a matter for conjecture. The expedition was considered a success and it assisted his standing.

He would be away for the better part of eight months in 1875–76 and spent half of that time in India. He was a relative progressive, in that on his return to London he protested to the government about the racial and religious prejudice that British administrators within the Raj would openly demonstrate. While not the final piece of the jigsaw, Benjamin Disraeli had promoted the trip as part of his plan to tighten the ties between Britain and India and have Victoria declared the empress of that colony.

There are other slightly more risqué similarities between William and Edward. The first had openly 'lived in sin' with an actress for twenty years. Edward would be married to Alexandra of Denmark in 1863 but before and after acquired a collection of mistresses and engaged in many one-night stands which risked scandal (and did land him in court in a divorce case involving adultery, which he denied). He was also fond of gambling and cards including baccarat (an illegal game at the time), which again dropped him in hot water when an argument over whether one participant, Colonel Sir William Gordon-Cumming, had been guilty of cheating got out of hand and resulted in embarrassing legal proceedings. Most of the time the public would indulge the prince, but not on that occasion.

Like William, he was not afraid of making loud pronouncements on prominent matters. He had to be talked out of speaking as a member of the House of Lords heartily in favour of the Third Reform Bill.

His salvation was his popular touch and easy temperament. He was more intelligent than he was credited for, but his true assets, as has been widely cited, were, like William IV, his charm and tact.

All of this makes a strong case that he, and not his mother, should be thought of as the founder of the contemporary constitutional monarchy.

His upbringing once he had escaped his father's regime would sound familiar to modern observers. He attended an array of universities, Edinburgh, Christ Church, Oxford, and Trinity

College, Cambridge. He never intended to sit for a degree (few gentlemen completed the course and took examinations then), but he did encounter some impressive tutors, attend lectures and acquire some genuinely valuable learning. The extensive travel in which he participated became the model for younger royals afterwards. He appreciated that the outside world was looking in on him and did not resent it. *Au contraire*, he consciously became an icon of men's fashion with a natty sense of dress, and he saw the new medium of photography as something to embrace, allowing him to establish his own image. His Middle East trip of 1862 was the first such venture to have an official photographer as part of the entourage. As the appetite for pictures of the royal family in the 1860s was considerable, and with his mother locking herself away in Windsor and Balmoral and not satisfying that demand, he stepped up to the plate.

The Prince of Wales actively revelled in public outings (again like William IV did), whereas George IV did not, and Victoria only came to tolerate them in her later years if conducted on her own terms. She wanted structure. He was at ease with spontaneity. Possibly because his mother would not allow him to do much else, he started the practice of senior members of the royal family opening buildings and bridges, the forerunner to the ribbon cutting that is the meat and drink of the House of Windsor. These activities would also invariably involve an element of performance and would always be photographed. Edward's audacious private life meant that he could not control everything that was said and written about him, but there was a strategy to all of this which included what we would dub media management.

The critical component was to be capable of engaging with people right across the spectrum and to be comfortable with an extremely extensive social circle, not a prisoner of protocol or court conventions. Edward did not want his sense of fun to be fulfilled wholly in private. It was he, in England, at least, who made horse racing the 'sport of kings', and the victories of his various thoroughbreds would being him pleasure that was clear to all those around him. In this, he had much in common with the masses. He was more a person of his time than his mother or father.

He also knew that it was important to get on with people. While his mother loathed Gladstone, her son was on far better terms. Edward went out of his way to cultivate friendships with Conservatives and Liberals, labour leaders such as Joseph Arch and even outright republicans. He had no problem with what some discounted as the nouveaux riches, with bankers aplenty among his intimates, a fair number of whom were Jewish, which attracted barbs from others. It did not bother him remotely. He applied the same dictum to his encounters with overseas statesmen of significance. His mother may not have wanted Garibaldi on British soil in 1864, but the Prince of Wales was entirely willing to meet him. In Paris, in 1871, he held talks and had lunch with Léon Gambetta, a man very much of the radical left.

On the basis of this preamble, it will come as no shock to see how he scores on the five key metrics.

Professional Standing

The new king started well in terms of acquiring a reputation for processing paperwork effectively. There had been a backlog caused by the ill-health, death and funeral of his mother (much as there was for William IV after the demise of George IV), but Edward had recruited talented people and the Buckingham Palace machine combined effectively with that of Whitehall and Westminster. Edward knew the major political players well and had relations with them which ranged from the close and cordial to the more formal and functional, but he did not have favourites as his mother did and nor, with the exception of the most radical and most reactionary ends of the spectrum, would he make enemies of MPs.

Edward VII (1901–10)

He had a ring-side seat at what was a fascinating hour in British politics. The Conservatives had once again prevailed in the general election of 1900 alongside their de facto coalition partners the Liberal Unionists, headed by Joseph Chamberlain, a man who combined left-of-centre views on social reform with right-of-centre opinions on the importance of empire (the second rather more important to him as the years went on than the first). Arithmetically, the Conservatives could do without Chamberlain's adherents in the House of Commons after 1900, in a way that would not have been feasible from 1895 to 1900, but the two camps were edging towards fusion and, in any case, Mr Chamberlain was an insurance policy. In 1902, the long-serving prime minister, Robert, Marquess of Salisbury, stood down to be succeeded by his nephew Arthur Balfour (hence the phrase 'Bob's your uncle'). Politics looked predictable.

In fact, it was about to ignite and it would provide a severe test of Edward VII's ability to keep some semblance of harmony in what over the next decade would become a very aggressive situation. Not long after Mr Balfour had kissed hands with the king, Mr Chamberlain announced that he believed the free trade gospel of the past sixty years or so to be either heresy or overtaken by events, and that tariffs (taxes on imports) were essential to prevent the further economic decline of the country. He campaigned for this among his own rank and file but more importantly sought to convert Conservatives.

This split the government and the wider Conservative Party in a manner not seen since Sir Robert Peel earned the hostility of his own party by agreeing to scrap the Corn Laws in the face of mass starvation in Ireland.

This was toxic terrain because there were strong reasons to suspect that tariffs would not appeal to a large section of the electorate. They would mean that foodstuffs, notably bread, would be more costly. They also meant the disavowal of what had seemed like a settled consensus. Winston Churchill crossed the floor to join the Liberals, such was the force of his disagreement with where policy appeared heading.

This internal feud paralysed the incumbent administration. In what might look like an extraordinary move (because it was), Balfour resigned and suggested that the king invite the Liberal leader, Henry Campbell-Bannerman, to form a government, despite not having a majority in the Commons. The hope was that the Liberals would take the bait and seek to introduce Home Rule in Ireland, an issue on which their membership was fixated (and had been for two decades) but which was also very unpopular.

The new prime minister was too shrewd to fall into that trap. He asked the king for a dissolution of Parliament. Edward VII theoretically might have refused, or sought to find another Conservative willing to assemble a Cabinet, but he stuck to the formbook and an election was held at the outset of 1906 in which the Liberals avoided any deliberation of Irish Home Rule (an electoral liability) and trained their fire on the Conservative stance on tariff reform, winning a smashing majority. The new administration then set upon a programme of social reform which the remaining Conservatives in the House of Commons sought to stymie but which their colleagues in the Lords were wary of blocking.

This did not strain the system too drastically. The road to a reckoning came in 1908 when Campbell-Bannerman departed the scene through illness, and Herbert Asquith was the natural successor. In one of the rare mistaken moves in the course of his duties, Edward VII did not cut short his annual break in Biarritz to oversee the change of prime minister, but had Asquith come to him instead.

Asquith, who had been the chancellor previously, appointed David Lloyd George, a figure aligned to the more radical wing of the Liberals, to that portfolio. Lloyd George faced a fiscal conundrum, in that he needed additional revenue to fund the old-age pensions scheme that the government had set up, but also required more money to expand the Navy, which he personally, along with Churchill, disagreed with.

This set the stage for the 'People's Budget' of 1909 and a constitutional showdown with echoes of the problems that William IV had endured with the Great Reform Bill some seventy-five years previously.

Lloyd George needed to find £16 million, a very sizeable amount of money. He raised income tax (which most people were too poor to pay) and added a super-tax for the richest slither of the population. He increased death duties on estates over £5,000. He brought in a new land tax. The least populist part of the package was the imposition of heavier taxes on tobacco and spirits, with the liquor licence duties also raised (although this went down well with many of the nonconformist teetotal Liberals).

It was by the standards of the day a radical financial statement, but the Liberals had a massive edge in the House of Commons and the accepted convention was that the House of Lords would not reject a money bill. Although their numbers in the House of Commons were small, the Conservatives set out to frustrate the government by procedural means, consuming the entirety of parliamentary time and ultimately requiring the Liberals to use drastic methods to ram the Budget through. The political temperature in the country as a whole increased, with a Budget Protest League established by the Conservatives and a Budget League created by the Liberals, and Lloyd George and Churchill engaging in the language of class war to such a level that the king asked Asquith to restrain them.

The Lords then went for the nuclear option in November 1909. They threw out a money bill and by a 350–75 margin. Asquith sought a dissolution and an election on the matter. The king accepted this.

The prime minister then made a mistake that would complicate the king's life considerably. In the opening speech of the contest, at the Albert Hall no less, he intimated that he had obtained a pledge from the king that if the Liberals won the election and the House of Lords continued to obstruct the Budget, then Edward VII would, *in extremis*, create enough new peers to make up a majority for it.

This is not what the monarch had pledged in secret discussions. He had suggested that if all else failed and the Liberals won a further general election after the one that was currently taking place, then he would sanction a wave of new peerages. He had not, as Asquith had hinted, agreed to take that step immediately.

The January 1910 election produced a hung parliament but with the Liberals and their allies in the ascendent. The government was now determined not merely to see the Budget become law, but to enact legislation to prevent any future misuse of money bills by the Upper House, to allow legislation which the Lords had rejected to become law automatically after two years, and to reduce the maximum term for the House of Commons from seven years to five years. This would be the next political frontline.

The House of Lords acknowledged the changed situation by allowing the Budget to pass without a division in April 1910. The king did not have to confront the mass production of new peers on this subject, but it looked increasingly probable that he might have to do so in a forthcoming clash on the Lords' powers.

We will never know exactly what he would have done because he died on 6 May 1910. The balance of probability is that he would have imposed another general election as a single-issue plebiscite on the proposals to curtail the authority of the Lords and, if that had been won, would have made it clear that he would flood the second chamber if they did not give way. They probably would then have surrendered (which is basically what happened under his successor but in a less than elegant way). If so, he would have repeated the formula that William IV settled on, consistent with his high professional standing. He sensed what a constitutional monarchy was. Such an episode under Victoria makes one shudder.

Public Opinion

Edward had usually been a popular Prince of Wales and there was widespread relief when it was confirmed that he had recovered from his bout of typhoid fever in 1871. He pushed his luck when his involvement with an illegal card school came to light and he had to take no more chances on that front. Self-restraint on women, song and cards (his wine consumption was limited but his fervour for cigars and cigarettes had few bounds) did not come easily to him, but self-preservation was a top priority.

He was even more popular as king. He maintained the style and tone that he had as Prince of Wales. There were enormous crowds at his coronation, and he attracted vast numbers of spectators at any of his public appearances. He was completely at ease with himself in the public arena. When he died, the mourning was intense and respectful to the boundary of reverential. An astounding convoy of more than 400,000 people filed by his coffin when he lay in state, a number probably not exceeded until the death of Elizabeth II, and his was an age in which it was hard to take time off work for travel. If public opinion alone were the metric of monarchy, then Edward VII would be in a class of his own.

Financial Competence

As was true for Edward's mother, the age in which the monarch was charged with the monetary state of the nation had long since receded into history. The only standard here is whether the way in which his own finances were organised strengthened or weakened his reputation (and this is marginal). As it happens, he was a rare example of an heir to the throne who became the monarch while in credit. His funding was sound, and he had a network of bankers to offer him the best advice in the business. He donated Osborne House on the Isle of Wight to the nation. Whether this was a gesture of generosity, a tribute to his mother, or because he could not bear the place himself is a subject for speculation.

Foreign Policy

Although the monarchy could not long take charge of foreign policy, Edward had an influential voice and was much more likely to be heeded than his mother. It was of utility to the government that he was an international celebrity, was affable, had travelled widely throughout his adult life, spoke French and Germany extremely well and was intrigued by how politics overseas operated. He also had some well-formed views on military matters, but they were concerned with internal features, not whom Britain should shoot at. He did, however, have reservations about his cousin Wilhelm II of Germany which would be validated.

He was a willing diplomat. He made an acclaimed state visit to France in 1903 (despite the fact that the coronation oath which he took included a passage in which he claimed to be King of France; that text would not be altered until George V received the crown in 1911). The British government wanted an alliance with France, which would be no mean feat after centuries in which the two territories had often clashed. His trip was an immensely valuable stepping stone to the *Entente Cordiale* which emerged in 1904. This was a considerable pivot when allowing not only the long past enmity, but also that there would be many parts of the world where the two countries were rivals for colonial influence and could not avoid continuing to be.

The personal touch of the king became embedded in British strategy. In what was then seen as quite a whirlwind way,

Edward VII made state visits to Athens, Oslo and Stockholm which all went very well. He felt obliged to confer with Wilhelm II in Berlin, which was an uneasy encounter, as much of the German press, amplifying the mindset of the political elite there, believed that behind the smiles the king and his ministers were determined to constrain their country. He also had an audience with Pope Leo XIII, which must have been of some symbolic value to his Roman Catholic subjects and particularly with Ireland seething with anti-British agitation, though not much of it directed at the monarch personally.

He also met with the Russian tsar on their yachts in what is now Tallinn in Estonia in 1908. That was a less pleasing sight to some on the political left in Britain as Nicholas II was not loved in that quarter. Until the end of his life, Edward was intrigued (and a little alarmed) by the state of Europe but placed less weight on the empire strung across the globe, including India. He was referred to as 'Edward the Peacemaker'. Nothing he could have done, even if he had survived longer, would have allowed one man to keep the peace.

He also had a serious input into the defence of the realm. He was very actively engaged with naval matters, which had become politically and practically more salient as it became less apparent that Britannia continued to rule the waves, however loudly that anthem was heard across music halls. He threw his support behind Sir John Fisher, a root-and-branch moderniser of the fleet, whose agenda was being frustrated by the more orthodox Establishment (mainly out of their self-interest). The Liberal government did not see this as unsolicited interfering. His status aided their own cause.

Much the same applied to the Army. The Boer War had revealed that all was not well within it. The British Army had not moved with the times, and this was exposed in South Africa by a small but well-marshalled band of opponents. The basic literacy and numeracy of the lowest ranks was dire (a new Education Act in 1902 was the direct result of what had been revealed) and the event had illustrated the public health difficulties experienced by the working classes. Britain had not fought a land war in the European theatre for almost 100 years. It would not be properly ready for one come 1914. Edward was associated with a zeal for reform. Once again, this was not seen as outside his station. He was an acclaimed figure who punched above his weight in foreign and national security matters.

Succession

Edward and his extremely devoted queen ensured that there would be no uncertainty about who came after them. They had six children, although one died very soon after birth, to the distress of his father. Their eldest son, Edward, Duke of Clarence, was lost to pneumonia at the tender age of 28, which was an appalling calamity for both of his parents. He had been engaged to Mary of Teck. His brother George would replace him as Prince of Wales and then himself be wed to Mary not long afterwards.

Succession should also be about stewardship. There was not much of that in how Victoria handled Edward. He took the diametrically opposite approach to George, once he was heir apparent. They were exceptionally close, and the king made more of an effort to prepare his son for what was to come than any monarch previously. As a rule, British kings and queens have been reticent about admitting their immortality. Edward was a very different figure in this regard. This should cement his reputation, less as a playboy prince (although there is plenty in that which is true) than as a conscientious and creative king and a badly underrated person.

Postscript

Elizabeth II (1952–2022)

It is inevitable that Elizabeth II will be best remembered many years hence for her long reign and even longer life. She broke more records in this regard than even the most successful Olympic competitors. To sit on the throne for seventy years and to remain broadly healthy until the age of 96 is astonishing. It is testament to her, and the extent to which it was hard for many to conceive of anyone else being their sovereign, that her end when it came appeared to be something of shock, despite her advancing years. Her husband had, after all, reached 99 years of age and her mother, 101.

A long reign is not, of necessity, an effective or outstanding one. The argument against the standing of Victoria has been made already. If there had been chapters on George III and Henry III, they would not have been flattering. Only Edward III hits the fifty-year or more mark as king with upbeat reviews. That Elizabeth II is also, ultimately, to be accorded the same with twenty years more on the clock is impressive. It was by no means certain or, at moments, even probable that this would transpire.

Elizabeth was not born to be queen. She came into this world not in a palace or a castle but in Bruton Street in Mayfair on

21 April 1926. She was the first born not to the heir to the throne (Edward, Prince of Wales) but to the second (Albert, Duke of York) and his wife, the Duchess of York (formerly Lady Elizabeth Bowes-Lyon). It was assumed at her arrival that the future Edward VIII would take a (respectable) wife and produce children of his own to secure the succession. This remained the hope even after the death of George V in January 1936, when the new king was certainly young enough to have found an appropriate princess from a Protestant country (although the options were not as multiple on that front as they had been in 1913) and to have had his own sons or daughters. Those on the political inside, however, would have been aware of what a sharp change in direction this would have to be for a man who had long enjoyed amorous engagements with married women, which did not much please his father, and that he was not the sort of character to be told he had to grow up.

Elizabeth was, therefore, for some while much closer to a presumed 'spare' than an 'heir'. She was not trained to be a monarch. Her education was predominantly organised by her mother with an emphasis as much on social skills as academic acclamation. The same was true for her younger sister, Margaret. It was only in December 1936, when her father was catapulted onto the throne as George VI, almost certainly past the point when he and the new queen might have another (male) child, that Elizabeth became the heir presumptive. Her life ahead would be transformed by this event.

It is hard to overstate just how dramatic and traumatic the abdication of Edward VIII was for the monarchy. There had been nothing quite like it in English history (Scotland had the flight of Mary, Queen of Scots, a departure strongly linked to another ill-advised marriage). It had come suddenly, with Albert/George only becoming fully aware of his fate as future king in the final weeks of his brother's short tenure. It was unclear whether anyone of standing might back Edward's offer to stay on as king but under the strictures of a morganatic marriage, whereby any children would be excluded from the throne. It turned out that only Winston Churchill as a figure of the first tier would be tempted, but he was a maverick then.

The attitude of the public at large was unpredictable. There was no blueprint or template for how an abdication might work and for dealing with all sorts of side effects that came into the equation. George VI had to buy Balmoral and Sandringham from his brother because they were owned by the royal family, not the nation, and Edward as the eldest son had received them through his father. What was such a figure, as an ex-king, to be called? (The title Duke of Windsor seems to have been plucked out of thin air.) If he did marry, would his wife be Her Royal Highness? (The answer was 'no,' to Edward's huge chagrin.) Where would such a person live? (Abroad, logically, but that would have to be sorted.) When could they be in England? What were they allowed to do when in the country? What happened if, later on, Edward was to regret his decision to depart relatively willingly and see himself as a latter-day James II, heading an alternative court in exile? (Mercifully, he did not have his own James III to come after him.)

To a degree that we cannot appreciate today, Princess Elizabeth was heir presumptive to what had the potential to be a legitimacy crisis. There were two kings out there. The younger one was now on the throne, but the older one (with the historic bloodline claim) was available, not in a monastery. He was the centre of international attention still – especially in the United States, courtesy of his wife. The new king was known not to be in the best of health, was shy and openly battled with a stammer. There were many in high places who were concerned about whether he could withstand the rigours of being king. His queen was aware of his frailties, and must have had doubts. Perhaps he did too.

Jumping a generation to a 10-year-old girl was no solution. Her status as the rightful heir had to be reinforced if the continuity and coherence of the monarchy were to be credible. It was mooted that she might be made Princess of Wales (George VI shot down that notion), but father, mother and daughter had been placed under an intense strain because Edward VIII had picked love over duty.

To understand how Elizabeth II should be assessed, ahead of the deployment of the five metrics for a monarch, it is vital to appreciate three aspects of her tenure. The first is how deep the deep end was that she was thrown into at the age of 25 when she became the sovereign. The second is that, although the scars of the abdication had mostly healed, the model of which the British monarchy was an entrenched version was a precarious one, almost without parallel in the world, a balancing act which throughout her reign would be a challenging one to maintain and which even today is the single most significant dilemma for the House of Windsor in the years ahead. The third aspect, which results in part from the first and notably the second, is that this lengthy reign had some striking highs and lows, not only for the queen personally, but for the institution that she led.

The Second World War was a blessing and a curse for the new monarchy. It resolved any lingering legitimacy crisis, in that the performance of the king and queen when the conflict came could not be faulted. Having made an awful error of allowing themselves to be too closely associated with appeasement through Neville Chamberlain's spectacularly misjudged invitation to the Buckingham Palace balcony after the Munich Agreement of 1938, George VI accepted Winston Churchill (nemesis on two fronts, having opposed Chamberlain and supported Edward VIII in late 1936) as prime minister and struck up warm terms with the most senior Labour Party members of the War Cabinet. The queen was the toast of the East End of London (and elsewhere) during the Blitz. Princess Elizabeth offered her first radio broadcast in 1940 on the BBC's *Children's Hour* and would later sign up at the age of 18 to the Auxiliary Transport Service (the king was doubtful, but it was the making of her as future queen). The Duke of Windsor, by contrast, acted in a fashion that brought reasonable suspicion of his loyalty. What to do with him in the early 1940s was a distraction. There would be no lobby for him in 1952. These were all blessings. The curse was that it was hard to train Elizabeth to be queen in these conditions.

The death of the king (while Princess Elizabeth, Duchess of Edinburgh, and the Duke of Edinburgh were in Kenya en route to Australasia) was still a thunderbolt. George VI was plainly not well but seemed to have recovered from a serious bout of illness in 1951, making his daughter's royal tour safe to proceed. He slipped away in his sleep at Sandringham. He was the youngest serving monarch to die since King Charles II in 1685. In an ironic twist, that king had no offspring of his own but a wayward younger brother with two daughters. George VI had a wayward elder brother but two daughters of his own. Elizabeth II was the youngest monarch to succeed since Victoria, who was just over 18 years old, but Victoria had spent much of the reign of the elderly William IV well aware that she could be called on.

The queen had to return to England to receive sincere commiserations (George VI was genuinely loved by this time) and to prepare for a coronation. One delicate matter was what to rebrand the former Queen (Consort) Elizabeth as, with the complication that she and her daughter shared the same first name. In ordinary times, this would have been relatively simple. The concept of dowager queen existed. The recently widowed queen appeared too young for that title; besides which, Queen Mary, the consort of George V, was then still alive (she died in early 1953) and she was the dowager queen (Britain had shifted from having a king and an ex-king to a queen and two queen consorts plus that ex-king). In an act of improvisation which lasted for fifty years, the idea of a 'queen mother' was alighted on.

Finding an appropriate role for her mother was one matter. Identifying another one for her husband was another. This raised more difficulties than one might imagine in our times (although television via *The Crown* has, in its highly exaggerated form, shed some light on the fact that there was an issue).

The marriage of Elizabeth to Philip was not applauded at every level. What to do with male consorts has proved sensitive. Mary Tudor's marriage and co-monarchy with Philip II of Spain was unpopular. Elizabeth I's refusal to wed avoided the matter but at the cost of an endless succession worry. Mary II was in the abstract the equal of William III and what you thought of him depended on whether you thought that 1688–89 was a Glorious Revolution or a Squalid Coup. Prince George of Denmark was a less contentious player, but that was because he accepted an almost humiliatingly humble position. Victoria's Albert was slated as the 'pauper prince', charged with being the power behind the throne.

Elizabeth did not start from a much better place. Philip was a relative (either a second cousin once removed or a third cousin, depending on how this is assessed). He was the son of Prince Andrew of Greece, who had been driven abroad in 1922. He had been entrusted to the Mountbatten family, who had sought to Anglicise him as best they could. He had needed to acquire British nationality for his war service and to build a life thereafter. Other members of his family had made the opposite set of choices and thrown in their lot with Nazi sympathisers. On that basis, he had three sisters who, it was felt, could not be invited to his wedding. He was relatively poor. Elizabeth had fallen for him at a very young age (her father had played for time by denying the prospect of an engagement until she had reached the age of 21). A title also had to be identified for him (that of Duke of Edinburgh emerged). He would not actually become Prince Philip until 1957. Finally, what was he to do in terms of royal activities?

Elizabeth II thus started her tenure younger than she was entitled to anticipate, with an awkward ex-king of an uncle still around, a restless mother, a husband who was not an immediate asset, and two very young children. She also acquired a model of monarchy with some significant drawbacks to it.

After Farouk of Egypt was deposed in 1952 (five months after Elizabeth II had ascended her throne), with the monarchy in his country abolished outright eleven months later (at about the same time as the coronation took place in Westminster Abbey), he complained and exclaimed that 'the whole world is in revolt'. A compulsive attender of casinos wherever he could find them (which may have been a factor in his overthrow), he wittily observed: 'Soon there will be only five kings left – the King of England, the King of Spades, the King of Clubs, the King of Hearts and the King of Diamonds.'[10]

Strictly speaking, this was not entirely right as England was the United Kingdom and had a queen, not a king (unless Farouk had meant Edward VIII, which whom he would have very easily bonded). The essence of his comment had ballast, nonetheless; in the 1950s, monarchs were in short supply.

This was manifestly the situation in Europe. The French monarchy, once the finest on the continent, had long ago vanished. The Russian one had collapsed during the Great War, moved out and then massacred by the Bolsheviks. Those of Germany and Austro-Hungary could not survive the defeat of 1918. Spain's ruling family was removed in the 1930s (but would come back). Lesser dynasties such as the Italian fell over after 1945; the Greek monarchy would finally be shuttered in 1967. Only those of Benelux and the Nordic countries remained, but they were light on pomp and in their status.

If not in fairness an anomaly, the British monarchy could be seen as idiosyncratic. It was not just (almost) one of a kind in number. It was, it remained, and it remains one of a kind institutionally. Elizabeth had to devote much of her reign to dealing with an extremely curious structure.

---

[10] *Oxford Essential Quotations* (6th edition), edited by Susan Ratcliffe (2018).

The core of the conundrum was, and is, this. There are broadly three types of monarchical model.

The first comprises a set where the monarch (invariably male) is not only the official head of state but, in reality, head of government as well. They have an authority that William IV would recognise. There are parliaments and prime ministers, but the writ of the king (or emir, or similar) runs large. They are in charge – until revolution does for them, as with Farouk in Egypt. There are not a lot of examples of this left, but they are concentrated in the Middle East plus Morocco. There is one more in Eswatini (the name of what was Swaziland since 2018), where Mswati III, who started his reign in 1986, is an absolute monarch (as he is allowed fifteen wives concurrently and has at least forty-five children, the country is spoilt for choice when it comes to succession). This was once true in Lesotho as well, where Letsie III has been the ruler since 1996, but squabbling between him and his father as to who might hold the title (Letsie is on his second stint) and an interim period of military rule have meant that, for most of the past thirty years, Lesotho has been a strictly constitutional monarchy with a weak king.

The second type of monarchy constitutes those where the monarch is a semi-divine figure totally detached from politics. They exist as an emblem of national consciousness, and if they do become involved in public life, it is invariably a recipe for trouble. They may or may not have a strong link with a particular religion. This is the standard for some nations in East Asia, such as Japan, Bhutan, Nepal and Thailand. Cambodia, because of its utterly wretched history in the 1970s, is a strange variation on this, in that it has a king (Norodom Sihamoni since 2004) who has nominal authority over what is really a one-party state.

The final category is what might be termed the citizen monarchies of Benelux and the Nordic countries. The monarch's formal role in politics is very limited (often they are shielded from it entirely or brought in at the last minute to formalise what the politicians have finalised) and these are secular countries. The purpose of these monarchies is to represent the country to itself and the outside world, to be symbolic and to a very large degree 'ordinary', rather than something with magic and mystery built into it. The restored monarchy in Spain was not initially meant to be of this form (Franco would not have left that behind) and was politically critical in its early years (with King Juan Carlos vigorously backing the return of democracy and EU membership, staring down an attempted uprising with aplomb in 1981), but since his abdication, the Spanish royals have actively sought to shift to a more Swedish formula.

Then there is the British monarchy, which Elizabeth II had to work with and around (as does her son). It is a hybrid. The constitutional doctrine of 'the Crown in Parliament' means that the monarch still appoints ministers (including the prime minister), opens Parliament and has to sign legislation for it to be valid, although the chances of casting a veto are zero. If there were to be an election that led to a badly hung House of Commons, the Palace would have to make some controversial decisions.

The queen was also (as the monarch has been since 1559), the Supreme Governor of the Church of England, an Anglican in that domain, a presbyterian in Scotland and, rather uncomfortably, also a defender of all faiths and none elsewhere. Elizabeth had to reconcile being a head of state with an uncharted expectation that, as elsewhere in Europe, she would also be a head of society. Tricky.

That would never make for a smooth flight for a full seventy-year duration. The bumps would be made more disturbing by the emergence by the 1980s of a massively more intrusive media. The royals adopted public relations (reluctantly on the part of the queen) but would always play second fiddle to the print press itself.

The queen can be said to have had a strong 1950s; a more mixed 1960s, as she struggled to find a place in the 'swinging sixties'; a better 1970s, as shown by the triumph of the Silver

Jubilee; a rollercoaster 1980s, as the Princess Diana effect came to light; an often dire 1990s, when some personal mishaps, the implosion of the marriages of her children and the division, divorce and death relating to the Princess of Wales threw everything up in the air, bringing her own relevance into the spotlight for the first time; a substantial recovery in the first decade of the new century, captured by the scenes of affection during her Golden Jubilee in 2002; and a full-blown zenith from then on, with a Diamond Jubilee in 2012 and a Platinum Jubilee in 2022, in which she could not play as full a part as she might have wanted, commemorated a few months before she passed away. By then she was the grandmother and great-grandmother not just to a family but to a nation and others elsewhere.

With this landscape drawn, how does Elizabeth II fare on the measures of monarchy?

Professional Standing

Elizabeth II always had a high professional standing during her reign and at times the unbridled respect of her peers. Her devotion to her work was consistently outstanding. She had, as time went on, unmatched experience which she could draw on. She would cooperate with fifteen UK prime ministers, the last of whom, Liz Truss, was for a matter of two days – but then again, Truss would only be in office for Charles III for less than seven weeks. Across the Commonwealth, the queen had working arrangements with about 170 heads of government. It was impossible to top that tally.

There were some rougher edges to this. She had sought to place her husband in command of her coronation rather than the hereditary occupant of that role (the Earl of Arundel). On most issues, the powers that be were more mighty at this illustrious ceremony than the upstart Duke of Edinburgh, although he is awarded high regard for allegedly being the loudest voice for televising the service. For most of her earliest years, the ageing Winston Churchill (in his 'Indian Summer' stretch as her prime minister until 1955) was more than willing to act as Lord Melbourne had done with Victoria. The dialogue with Anthony Eden was cooler and she felt excluded from the discussion over Suez.

She would receive some criticism when Mr Eden fell on his sword over that Suez Canal debacle. She found herself in the warped place of having to choose, in effect, a prime minister and a Conservative Party leader, which appeared to smack of the monarchy of yesteryear, not of a post-war form. What made it more inconvenient was that there was a contest between Rab Butler and Harold Macmillan, and it was totally opaque as to who the returning officer should be and how support for the contenders should be divined. Churchill wanted to keep out Butler (who had been an arch-appeaser as late as the summer of 1940), and the youthful monarch appeared to be his instrument.

This would be deeper quicksand when Harold Macmillan retired due to supposed ill-health in 1963 (only to keep breathing until 1986). This time the fight was more open, but the rules of the game were even more undefined. Mr Butler was still in the ring and had some strong admirers. There were other contenders, such as Lord Hailsham and, as an outside possibility, Reginald Maudling, a fresh-faced chancellor. The Earl of Home, the foreign secretary, was supposed to be one of those who were guiding the process, rather than being part of it; as a member of the House of Lords, he was thought functionally disqualified. Yet what was later condemned as a 'Magic Circle' of senior Conservatives (who would never forget or forgive the Rab Butler of 1940) managed to manufacture a black ball for the man who had appeared as the front-runner and Elizabeth II was convinced to send for Home as prime minister. On the basis of the counsel that she had received, and with the reticence of the

Conservative Party to do anything to assist her by holding a swift advisory ballot of its own MPs, she acted correctly. It did not, though, leave the best of impressions that the country had an earl in 10 Downing Street who had to renounce his peerage and create a by-election to enter the House of Commons in late 1963, where he would be denounced by a dynamic new Labour leader, Harold Wilson, as the '14th Earl' (although it has to be conceded that the '14th Earl' nearly defeated Wilson in 1964).

There would not be a similar disagreement to ensnare Elizabeth II for a very long time afterwards. The closest was when it was reported that she had a testy time with Margaret Thatcher, most starkly concerning the government's resistance to imposing sanctions on South Africa over apartheid, but also for the tenor of her conduct of domestic policy. This was a catalyst for comment, but it stayed mostly suppressed. It would not be particularly destabilising.

When the crisis came, it was volcanic. The death of Princess Diana in 1997 in a car crash in Paris was, to begin with, appallingly mishandled. The queen was away in Balmoral, as were Prince Charles and his two young children, and it was considered to be best to keep them secluded in Scotland. That was understandable. The instinct that the princess should be subject to a Spencer family funeral was completely misplaced. So was the lack of a response to huge crowds, mountains of flowers and very evident grief in the middle of London. Tony Blair, as prime minister, had to press the queen to switch course while his right-hand man, Alastair Campbell (an improbable defender of the monarchy) sought to change the national narrative. A well-delivered television broadcast (essentially an apology) on the evening before the funeral lowered the temperature. Elizabeth II would not be caught out ever again. Even potential 'bouncers', such as how to adapt to political devolution in the UK, did not upset her.

Public Opinion

Elizabeth II was highly rated by the public at large throughout her reign and that tended to hold true consistently across her tenure and incredibly strongly in her last years. Perhaps the main exception is those first few days of September 1997, which were unforgettable for all.

There were some other missteps, too. The queen was slow to be seen at the sight of the Aberfan tragedy, where 116 children perished, in 1966. The decision to permit the filming of the television documentary *Royal Family* in 1969 probably falls under the 'good idea at the time' heading and would legitimise media intrusion at a later stage. The revelation in 1979 that the person responsible for her art, (ex-Sir) Anthony Blunt, had been a Soviet spy, recruited while an undergraduate at Cambridge in the 1930s, was a serious embarrassment too.

However, where there was most volatility was in the ratings of the royal family as a whole and, on some occasions, the monarchy as an institution. The private life of Princess Margaret, with a marriage denied and another one that culminated in divorce, was a frequent source of attention. This would be insignificant compared with the soap opera that was the end of the fairy-tale union of her heir Charles and Lady Diana Spencer, who in separation and divorce became a force all of her own, and the squalid sequel of Prince Andrew and Sarah Ferguson (Andrew, by then Duke of York, would cause her a great deal of public relations turbulence in the final decade or so of her tenure). Princess Anne also saw her marriage dissolved, in a more dignified manner, but held on to public respect. Other more minor royals kept newspaper circulation ticking over. Elizabeth's husband, Prince Philip, was more than capable of creating his own set of gaffes, but he did not imperil the monarchy as he was semi-detached from it.

The queen managed to stay above the fray, and played an effective long game in terms of public opinion.

Financial Competence

As with Edward VII and Victoria (and even William IV), the world had changed too much for the monarch to be responsible for the national finances, which is just as well in consideration of the nadir experienced in the 1970s. As with those other monarchs, how Elizabeth managed their own (taxpayer-assisted) funding mattered.

This was probably the weakest spot in the measurement of her monarchy but was not entirely her own fault. Others were plainly reluctant to tell her what she might not have wanted to hear. It was also a consequence of the complex hybrid of monarchy that the UK had established. A wider royal family would trigger arguments about who got what, for what, and much it should be.

The antics of the queen's children and some random pieces of bad luck were unhelpful. A fire at Windsor Castle in 1992 (part of what Elizabeth II dubbed, in a rare instance of a Latin soundbite, her *annus horribilis*) served to prise open an unfortunate can of worms. Discussion about the Civil List burst into the open, along with an unattractive debate (from the queen's perspective) as to who was 'value for money'. Even the queen mother's apparently huge bank overdraft was not off-limits. The royal accounts had to be overhauled. Elizabeth 'volunteered' to pay income tax, technically to herself as it was Her Majesty's Treasury that obtained the receipts. Buckingham Palace was to be opened to the public (at a charge) both as a modernisation initiative and to bring in more revenue. There was an on-off conversation about whether the royal yacht *Britannia* should be replaced. It was all a little sordid.

Foreign Policy

In the modern age, the notion that a monarch might have a role in foreign policy might seem archaic. Foreign policy issues had long since been devolved to the prime minister and the government.

In outline terms this is correct. The queen did not steer policy as regards the EEC/EC/EU or NATO.

This did not mean that she failed to be an asset. Far from it. She was a global brand throughout her life. This was worth something to British 'soft power', whose importance rose as its hard power sank. If the external world thought of the queen, they would think of the UK. That was of real currency.

Elizabeth was an astonishing traveller. In her first full year as queen, she went on a lengthy overseas tour (for months on end, with her young children left behind), involving thirteen countries and including Australia, where it is claimed that 75 per cent of the population turned out to glimpse her, and New Zealand. She would meet fourteen American presidents (Lyndon Johnson was the hold-out) and would be called up to cement the special relationship as required, even forcing Donald Trump to behave himself. Some of these visits were symbolic but others were very consequential. Her tour of the Republic of Ireland in 2011 and subsequent shaking of hands with Martin McGuinness, the IRA chief of staff turned Deputy First Minister of Northern Ireland, was seen as cementing a sensitive peace process.

It was the Commonwealth where the queen flew her colours the highest. It was close to a personal invention. It had consisted of seven countries (plus the UK) when she ascended the throne (Australia, New Zealand, Canada, South Africa, India, Pakistan and what was then called Ceylon). By the time of her death, it had reached fifty-six nations – some of which, like Mozambique and Rwanda, had never been in the empire. This expanse of humanity involved around a third of the world's population.

There were those, including some at the Foreign Office, who could not understand the utility of this organisation, but pointless clubs rarely attract an increase in membership. The queen was its steward. She risked friction with Margaret Thatcher over Rhodesia and then South Africa to keep it on the road. She would strike up an alliance with Nelson Mandela, the prisoner turned President of South Africa. Australia, a possible rebel on republicanism, would vote to retain her as head of state in late 1999.

This was heavy lifting. Queen Elizabeth made more than 200 tours of Commonwealth members. She attended seven different Commonwealth Games. She was there at twenty-two Commonwealth Heads of Government meetings. The last of these, in Malta, where she had lived as a young princess when her husband was still on active military service, convened in 2015, would be her final overseas visit as the UK monarch.

Succession

Her children may have been the cause of cringeworthy headlines, but succession was not an issue. She left a longstanding heir, Charles, who survived the Diana episode and a menace to his status. There was a second son, Prince Andrew (who was, however, badly damaged goods), and another in Prince Edward. Princess Anne was a well-admired daughter. Charles had secured his own succession with an elder son, William, who had two boys and a girl of his own by 2022, and a younger one, Harry, who would prove that the family problem with rogue members was not just a forgotten detail of history.

The succession was sombre but smooth. The new king was accepted by all but die-hard republicans. This might not have happened as it did had Elizabeth II not largely played a blinder in her last two decades on the throne. Eminent historians, including Norman Davies, an authority with little equal in the eyes of this writer, had thought in 1999 (just before the vote in Australia, which Elizabeth II was deemed likely to lose) that the writing was on the wall for the House of Windsor. Before too long, if it was 'difficult to guess when the final blow would fall', probably when the queen died, they were 'bound to join their relatives the Hohenzollerns and the Romanovs, on one of the various ex-royal circuits'.[11]

That has not happened. Elizabeth II's greatest gift was to allow Charles III to succeed to the throne and have the chance to be a bridge (much in the spirit of William IV and Edward VII) to a new age of constitutional monarchy, and for him in turn to permit a future William V the space and time to consider how to shift the UK completely over to a citizen monarchy, so that it might yet enter the twenty-second century.

---

11 Norman Davies, *The Isles: A History* (1999), p. 786.

Conclusions on Crowns

There are so many observations that one could make about the material contained in these pages, and conclusions which could be drawn about the monarchy and the nature of leadership more broadly. An exercise which starts in 1066 and ends by wondering what the monarchy might look like in 2066 is an innately and inevitably ambitious enterprise. There is the risk of reading too much into too much. However, to end without some concluding thoughts, which others can consider and contest, would be cowardly, even if this risks the possibility of those inclined to accept the arguments so far getting buyer's remorse.

Five general but intriguing themes, the author believes, can be articulated in these pages, as well as a defence of, and contemplation related to, the five measures of monarchy that have been utilised.

The first is that we tend to think of British history (for which read 'English', too often) as a continuum starting with William I and progressing on, admittedly with deviations, through to the present day.

In terms of the jurisdictions in which monarchy has occurred, this is not an accurate analysis at all.

The years that are covered within these chapters actually fall into (at least) ten different phases:

1. A period when the story is one of England and France – but not all of England all of the time, as Cornwall could be semi-detached and there was the curious status of the prince bishops of Durham, who were mostly (but not entirely) a domain of their own from 1075 to 1536 (when Henry VIII reincorporated them in a rough manner). The boundary between England and Scotland was hardly reliable and secure, so who held what in the northern counties varied. Nor was 'France' what we consider to be France today. What those who were the King of England controlled there would change frequently, until Calais and then later on nothing.
2. An age when England and sections of France were combined with sections of the island of Ireland (crucially Dublin and the Pale) for the monarch. This started with the incursion made by Henry II in 1171 and was formally fused by Henry VIII in 1541 but stayed personal to him.
3. An era when England, moving parts within France and the most enticing counties of Ireland had bolted on to them the vast bulk of Wales as a result of Edward I's kingship (1272–1307).
4. A time (1558–1603) with all of the above but without any of France after Calais was lost.
5. A period of union of the Crowns of England and Scotland but not the merging of the two countries (1603–1707), with Wales now an adjunct of England, and Ireland in effect a separate domain.
6. An era when England (and Wales) had entered an Act of Union with Scotland but with the Irish still on the outside as a different but dominated country (1707–1801).
7. A time after the Act of Union with Ireland when a single nation existed (1801–1922).

8. A period following the division of the Republic of Ireland and Northern Ireland, with what was sometimes known as Eire breaking free, partially and then fully, and renouncing links to the empire and the Commonwealth, but with Northern Ireland uniquely having its own Parliament (1922–72).
9. A period of Great Britain and Northern Ireland in which direct rule of the latter from London was the norm (1972–99).
10. An era from 1999 in which devolution has developed, with the re-establishment of a Scottish Parliament and the creation of the Welsh Assembly (later Senedd), both with steadily accumulating authority, and an extraordinarily protracted, painful and political process by which a unique consociational arrangement was brought into being for Northern Ireland, but with lengthy suspensions and a continued lack of clarity about its endurance. This is the United Kingdom of the present day (at the time of writing), an example of asymmetric semi-federalism all of its own (and minus a single constitutional document which might conceivably make more sense of this mosaic).

These are strikingly different conditions in which a monarchy might be obliged to seek to operate, and they exclude the Commonwealth of 1649–60 which convulsed all of the countries cited above.

The second item to note is that the expectations of monarchs have also changed a lot over the centuries. National security either by attacking others or repelling invasion was once the primary function of those on the throne. More sophisticated tools of diplomacy and trade then came into the repertoire. There was also an evolution in the balance of power between the king or queen and the rest of the nobility, then between the Crown and Parliament, then within Parliament between the House of Commons and the House of Lords, and in the last two decades between the Westminster Parliament and the devolved ones, so that, for the most part but not absolutely, the influence of the monarch on fiscal affairs was marginalised to how they handled their own resources, not the national monetary stockpile, and their influence in foreign policy was diminished, though not extinguished. These were huge shifts (if perhaps not as confusing as the territorial features set out above) and they make comparisons between monarchs a task for the surgeon, not the most general of practitioners.

The third is that monarchical succession has proved extremely fragile. A simple process by which adult sons or daughters hand onto their first-born adult sons or daughters does not happen frequently. It is punctuated by monarchs passing the baton on their death to an adult who was not their first born, or to their brother, or a grandchild, or an even more distant relative, or to a minor of some type. Disrupted succession is more regular than the textbook example. Of the seven monarchs described in this book as 'overrated', William I, Richard I, Henry V, Henry VIII, Elizabeth I, William III and Victoria, none of them at the age of 5 would have been entitled to regard themselves as in line to be monarch. William had to seize the country. Richard I had older brothers. Henry V's father, Henry IV, was some distance from taking the plunge and pushing out Richard II. Henry VIII had Prince Arthur ahead of him. Elizabeth I had an older sister at the time of her birth and would soon have a younger brother ahead of her as well. William III was miles away from a scenario in which England (or a section of its elites) would recruit him to eject his father-in-law and then rule with his wife, and alone after her death. In 1824, Victoria, aged 5, had two uncles ahead of her.

It is almost the same for the seven monarchs considered to be underrated in this volume. To recap, these were Stephen, Henry II, Edward III, Henry VII, Anne, William IV and Edward VII. Stephen had the doomed Prince William in front of him until the *White Ship* was lost in 1120, then Matilda as a better bloodline heir and the small matter of an elder brother whom he had shoved rudely to one side. Henry II would initially also have Prince William as a superior claimant and then, if Stephen had entrenched himself on the throne, his sons Eustace and William as rivals *in situ*. Edward III was the eldest son of Edward II, but he was made to become a symbolic actor in a conspiracy that had his father removed from the throne and murdered, and to begin with he was a boy at risk of a sticky end. Henry VII's blood credentials for the throne were thinner than the man himself was, by all accounts. Anne was the second daughter of her father's first marriage and, for the purist, the birth of a son to James II in 1688 demoted her even further in the pecking order. William IV was the third brother and not a contender to be king at all until the (probably careless and needless) end of Princess Charlotte in 1817 moved him into the frame, but he was not firmly there until Frederick, Duke of York, died in 1827. Only Edward VII was a first-born child, an heir for life, who became king after a peaceful death.

Elizabeth II fits this pattern too, as at the time of her birth it was thought her uncle would provide an heir. There is a shocking amount of roulette (verging on the Russian variety) about who sits on the throne.

The fourth point to chew upon is how hard it is to form a new dynasty, and anyone who does so successfully has to have something that can be said for them. To do so without blood being shed as well, or the imminent threat of conflict, is an exceptionally unusual experience in England (and Scotland).

The case studies illustrate this compellingly. William I was never likely to follow Edward the Confessor without competition from others, and he had to snatch the Crown from Harold Godwinson (with a lot of luck in that endeavour). Henry II nearly had to fight Stephen to become king before an enlightened pact permitted him to be the initial Plantagenet monarch. The Lancastrian wing of that family would only become the pre-eminent line by the overthrow and the murder of a king, Richard II. The same would eventually prove true when the Yorkists struck back through the despatch of Henry VI. They would hang on to power temporarily by fratricide-meets-regicide as Richard III replaced Edward V.

The Tudors had to enhance their eminently disputable credentials to the throne at Bosworth Field, with Henry VII inconvenienced by rebellions thereafter. The Stuarts, essentially uniquely, took over without a serious whiff of strife, but this was no thanks to Elizabeth I. Of their number, however, Charles I would be deposed and executed (back to the customary routine) and James II later exiled. The House of Hanover was ushered on to the throne in 1714, without much acclaim, and had to confront one Jacobite invasion in 1715 and another thirty years later led by Bonnie Prince Charlie. The switch to the House of Saxe-Coburg-Gotha under Edward VII was window dressing in reality. The coming of the House of Windsor, to begin with in 1917 and then reaffirmed by the young Queen Elizabeth II in 1952 (to the ire of her husband, who preferred Mountbatten or Mountbatten-Windsor), was the equivalent, necessitated by the Great War, of respraying the paint on a car. Introducing a dynasty is tough (with a plainly slim blood claim, really tough), which is what makes Henry VII such an underrated figure.

All of the above leaves some intoxicating 'what ifs' in our monarchical history. There are many of these potentially, but here are twelve that might make the basis of another tome someday.

1. What if William I had nominated his eldest son, Robert (not William II), as his successor?
2. What if Prince William had not perished at sea in 1120 but lived on to replace Henry I?
3. What if Richard I had married Alice of France as soon as he could have done, rather than stringing out an engagement over two decades, and had had an heir before leaving on crusade?
4. What if Edward, the Black Prince, had not expired in 1376, a year before Edward III did?

5. What if Prince Arthur had not died in 1502, but had instead had issue, with Henry VIII never to be king?
6. What if either Edward VI or Mary Tudor had been in a position to have viable children?
7. What if Elizabeth I had succumbed to smallpox in 1562, opening a door for a Catherine I?
8. What if the best of Queen Anne's many attempts to have children, William, had not died in 1700?
9. What if in 1702, James, son of James II, had declared himself to be a Protestant convert?
10. What if Princess Charlotte, and perhaps even her stillborn son, had survived intact in 1817?
11. What if the assassination attempt on Queen Victoria (and Albert) in 1840, at the behest of Edward Oxford (the closest shave of her reign), had succeeded and her extremely unpopular uncle Ernest Augustus, Duke of Cumberland and Elector of Hanover, had moved on the throne?
12. What if Edward VIII had not been such a bounder and had either married earlier and had a child before reaching the throne in 1936, or walked away from Mrs Simpson and not his position?

This is more than enough to ponder. To wrap up, a final defence of the five measures of monarchy.

Professional Standing

Monarchy is not a one-man (or a one-woman) band. Reputation within elites truly matters. The best monarchs started from the basis that they needed to earn respect rather than demand it and showed some flexibility in being willing to include others in decision making if that strengthened their hand thereafter. The two most tyrannical (and hence overrated) figures covered in this text, William I and Henry VIII, did not think that these rules applied to them. One sucked the culture out of the English. The other launched a smash-and-grab raid upon the monasteries to fund his approach to marriage. Both preferred to do much of what they did via proxies (Odo of Bayeux principally for William the Conqueror, and Thomas Wolsey, Thomas Cromwell and to a degree Thomas Cranmer for Henry). This was because William was often defending his Normandy fiefdom and Henry VIII was often bone idle.

The best of monarchs had a completely different approach to their task and a better temperament. Stephen, for all of the many difficulties during his tenure, did take his duties extremely seriously. Henry II was often out of the country but had a deep interest in the quality of royal administration, the condition of local government and, above all else, the quality of the law and justice. The same holds for Edward III in spades. Henry VII could have launched his own MBA in Applied Monarchy. Anne had less power in her own hands but was diligent and sought to navigate choppy waters. William IV surpassed (perhaps not undemanding) expectations and rolled up his sleeves as king. Edward VII did the same with a much surer touch than his mother. These were all solid players.

Elizabeth II, as has been noted, was a thorough monarch from the outset, and by the end, even when well past nine decades in age, she was a sharper and shrewder soul than her younger prime ministers.

Professional standing is thus the basis of monarchical achievement. It is a stretch to come up with a good monarch, other than those assessed as underrated here, who did not pass this test with ease. The measure of monarchy is dialogue not dictatorship, detail not delegation, reform not reaction.

Public Opinion

This is the most challenging metric to stretch across a sizeable set of monarchs. The methods for evaluating it among the earliest of these figures is clearly imperfect (but there are indicators). This would be more enticing terrain if opinion polling had been invented in 1065 and used on a regular basis from then onwards. We have to work with the tools that we have, some of which are blunted.

This might matter less than it would appear. Public opinion becomes a weightier force as time moves on. It is completely safe to estimate that the innate English did not relish the Norman Conquest, that the absence abroad of Richard I and Henry V was noticed (even if their courage was commended), that Henry VIII had turned the national religion inside out to suit himself and that Elizabeth I was not married. A survey would not be needed to know that William III was a polarising individual or that Victoria almost vanished off the face of the Earth for a significant proportion of her long tenure.

The underrated were not always adored. Stephen (despite the carnage and chaos of a civil war) seems to have been. Henry II also clearly had a fan base. Edward III (until the last) inspired faith. Henry VII, with many other attributes, was not much of a crowd-pleaser (but was not hated either). Anne attracted fond sentiments. William IV had an element of the Elvis Presley to him. So did Edward VII.

In a much more constrained and restrained manner, Elizabeth II was a steadily acclaimed monarch. If a Charles III, William V and George VII are to extend the monarchy, they will need to be popular too. That must be achieved by dint of deed and empathy and not the dark arts of communications gurus, who can be too clever by half at times, to the longer-term detriment of their clients, royal or regular.

Financial Competence

This is a yardstick that changes over the years but never to the point that it did not matter one inch. In the early days, the monarch was absolutely central to fiscal policy and the health of the economy. It was possible to be overrated and yet effective in balancing the books (William I mostly was), but to be a bloodsucker not only on tax revenues but on much else too is not to win proper approval in history. In the underrated camp, Stephen was mostly hopeless in the financial space for the majority of his tenure (although he began well and finished with a spurt), but he had other sound virtues to him.

As a rule, however, overrated monarchs were bad overlords of finance. Richard I was never there to look at the books and had an astoundingly expensive crusade and then his own ransom to subsidise. Henry V was also an absentee figure whose passion for warfare never had price-tag limits attached to it. Henry VIII had none of his father's flair for figures and had debased the coinage (and a lot more) by the moment that he went to his deathbed. Elizabeth I certainly acquired some of that gene pool. Her legacy as the de facto chancellor of the Exchequer was not one to write home about it. William III was again far too fond of expensive combat, which increased taxation and undermined trade. Victoria no longer had a route into the bank, but her financial management of herself was unsteady.

The underrated (bar Stephen) do much better. Henry II was an astute organiser of public (and his own) finances. His successors would swiftly turn that into ashes. Edward III grafted here (but his grandson Richard II did not have the same qualities to him). Henry VII was a financial genius (yet this was not transferred to his successor either). Anne did nothing to hint at any personal extravagance. William IV conjured up success on a shoestring (the total opposite of George IV, his brother, before).

Edward VII was certainly aware of how to have a good time in life, but not at the expense of taxpayers.

Elizabeth II (his great-granddaughter) was not a high roller but there were many snouts in the trough during her reign. This was, as previously asserted, a relatively rare area where media jabs had genuine justification.

The power of the purse is potent. An intelligent monarch has an insight into their balance sheet.

Foreign Policy

Along with enhancing the domestic base by a high professional standing and financial acumen, the construction and content of foreign policy is pivotal to the standing of a monarchy. This did not stay the same over the centuries, as authority seeped first to Parliament and then the executive, but it was never redundant. It will not be immaterial for Charles III and those who come after him either.

It was once principally a matter of conducting war, although not all of the early monarchs saw combat as compulsory. It came to have a much more diplomatic component and the impact on trade and wealth rose in importance.

The overrated do not have much of a record to speak of in this sphere. For William I, England was his foreign policy in many respects, in that his interests in Normandy meant more to him than England. The newly suppressed country was there to exploit, so that he could flex his muscles all across France. Richard I was the last of the monarchs who charged out to the Third Crusade to realise that it was a fool's errand, and while out there he managed to alienate the King of France and the allies of the Holy Roman Emperor, so spent a year or more in prison while the tin was shaken at home to get him out. Not one to cut his losses, he then spent his last five years in a costly bid to take back French terrain. Henry V became obsessed with being King of France as well as England, but he had no blueprint as to how this might work if the title could be achieved and then retained. In turns, Henry VIII fell out with everyone: France, Spain, the Holy Roman Emperor and a few Popes.

Elizabeth I could scarcely afford to have a foreign policy, such was the condition of her finances. She tried to run a conflict with Spain by stealth, through the Spanish Netherlands and with nudge-nudge, wink-wink piracy, but almost came a cropper for it. The Armada was a Spanish defeat, not an English victory. Her determination not to marry meant that on her death, a foreigner would replace her. The whole tenure of William's time as king was defined by his desire to contain France (in order to assist Holland). Victoria and her husband were ineffective at making their preferences on foreign affairs into policy.

The underrated again rattle up the points here. That is less valid for Stephen in one sense, in that he hardly had a foreign policy at all but, at odds with William the Conqueror, his priority was England, not France, so disengagement from the internal politics of Normandy was probably a real blessing. Henry II was an outstanding diplomat (alas he found it hard to convince his feuding sons of this), who was capable of raising his sights beyond France and to a wider European canvas (he also resisted the slightest hint of a new crusade, which was rational of him). Edward III also had smart foreign policy aims, if mostly in France, and if he had died earlier, or the Black Prince had lived, he would have had more of a legacy. Henry VII spotted the coming of Spain, put the wool trade before warfare, had no romanticism about retaking France and found the best combination of friends and enemies. Anne wanted out of the War of the Spanish Succession and finally found her means of pulling that plug. William IV was a plus for Great Britain abroad. Edward VII was very much its diplomat.

Elizabeth II, in her own way, was on a par with William IV and Edward VII, and via her constant push to make the Commonwealth survive and thrive she had a personal imprint on international relations. She had more impact than Victoria ever did, even though she took to the throne 115 years later.

A positive effect on foreign policy is, therefore, a hallmark of an underrated king or queen.

Succession

As argued earlier in this concluding chapter, succession has often been the banana skin of monarchs. To some degree this is forgivable. They do not decide when they will die. They can seek to produce heirs, but fail despite valiant activity or have them predecease them. They can do their duty on this front well, only for their successors to waste what has been left them or fail to produce heirs of their own. Succession is to that extent a sweepstake. All a monarch can do is try the best that they can.

The distinction between the overrated and the underrated is thus less clear-cut on this measure.

William I did provide for succession, in that he left behind a set of male heirs. He also penned a will that would set Robert, who won Normandy but was excluded from England, and William II and then Henry I at loggerheads with one another. Richard I showed so little interest in marriage (he agreed to one eventually, but mainly because his mother was intent on it) and then children as to stoke some discussion as to whether he was more attracted to men than women (a reasonable choice today but awkward for a late twelfth-century monarch). Henry V left behind a boy of only 9 months in age (if he had remained in England or a protected base in Paris, this might not have been the case). Henry VIII created havoc in his desperate attempt to acquire a son, who nevertheless expired as a teenager. Elizabeth I simply went on strike regarding the succession, despite the woes that this would cause for England. William III was as apparently unconcerned about his childless status as was Richard I (possibly with similar external factors at play), so took the country down the road to the Act of Settlement, 1701. Victoria produced nine children, so is beyond reproach on this matter, but froze out poor Edward VII.

The underrated are a more random group on this essential but unpredictable aspect of monarchy.

Stephen's merit lies in that having lost his son, but with another in store, he sealed the deal with Henry II, and England escaped from a civil conflict that could have raged for many years longer. Henry II had many sons in his life and had two there by the moment of his death. It was not down to him that one favoured war over women and another had little to commend him on any level. It was not dissimilar for Edward III, who had an awesome heir apparent in Edward, the Black Prince, but he died and the hapless Richard II came to the throne as a boy after him. Henry VII had, by 1501, two sons and two daughters. Arthur's loss reduced that number to just one son, but this should have been sufficient. Anne could not have tried harder, was robbed by successive tragedies, but had an open mind about whether there could be a James III if he would only renounce Roman Catholicism. William IV had an army of illegitimate children and tried to rise to the occasion (as it were) once it was likely that he would become king, but despite a noble effort he was ultimately unsuccessful. Edward VII had sons and, atypically, was what we would call a mentor to his heir.

Elizabeth II had four adult children. They may have their faults, but succession was not the question. Her quest was to maintain the monarchy intact so that it was not agreed that it should end with her.

Professional standing, public opinion, financial competence, foreign policy and succession are, it will be contended one last time in this work, the five gold rings for effective monarchy. They are not an entirely perfect series of measures across what is a very long stretch of time, but they are valuable. They allow us to look at history in a different way. They reveal the overrated and the underrated. In modified form, they may be useful not only in assessing the past but in anticipating the future.

Further Reading

This book has been light on references to other works, in part because these can interrupt the flow of an argument, but also because the material presented has been accumulated over more than two decades and not meticulously recorded. Some of the research has involved individual monarchs but most of has been of a broader scope. Enthusiasts for histories of the British monarchy do not want for reading.

Those who have enjoyed this attempt at comparative history over a period of several centuries might be interested in the following ten volumes (although none of them are as comparative as this one).

The Isles: A History. Norman Davies (Papermac, 1999). Monarchy is but part of this immense and truly astonishing examination of the history of the British Isles. Highly recommended.

A Brief History of the British Monarchy: From the Iron Age to King Charles III. Jeremy Black (Robinson, 2022). An inevitably sweeping attempt by a highly respected academic to cover a vast space of time in a mere 256 pages.

The Shortest History of the Crown. Stephen Bates (Old Street, 2023). Ironically, despite its title, at 288 pages this is longer than the above tome. Very much a book of facts and one that concentrates on royal customs rather more than the relative performance of monarchs.

The Oxford Illustrated History of the British Monarchy. John Cannon/Ralph Griffiths (Oxford University, 1988). Deals with monarchy in this country from a long time before the Norman Conquest.

Crown and Sceptre: A New History of the British Monarchy from William the Conqueror to Charles III. Tracy Borman (Hodder & Stoughton, 2021). A scholarly offering which in the course of 576 pages covers every monarch of the period. Described in one review as being 'a synthesis of historical analysis, politics and top-notch royal gossip'. Not comparative in aim.

Kings and Queens of Britain, Illustrated History of: A Visual Encyclopedia of Every King and Queen of Britain, from Saxon Times through the Tudors and Stuarts to Today. Charles Phillips (Southwater, 2022). Does what it says on the tin through 500+ portraits and photographs.

The Lives of the Kings and Queens of England. Edited by Antonia Fraser (Weidenfeld and Nicolson, 1975). A little dated in style perhaps (not least in the reference to 'England' rather than 'Britain') but an intriguing set of short essays from William I onwards.

Kings and Queens of England and Scotland. Plantagenet Somerset Fry (DK Publishers, 2023). An extremely succinct (less than 100 pages) introduction to all the various monarchs.

Further Reading

Crown and Country: A History of England through the Monarchy.
David Starkey (Harper Press, 2010). As one might expect from
this author, an erudite and lengthy case for the monarchy
(it is a 'good thing'), and a compelling if by no means truly
comparative study.

*Kings, Queens, Bones and Bastards: Who's Who in the English
Monarchy from Egbert to Elizabeth II.* David Hilliam (The
History Press, 2004). A compendium which makes the most
of 'fascinating facts' about various kings and queens over
the centuries.

There are literally hundreds of other books about the individual
monarchs examined in this volume.

You may also enjoy ...

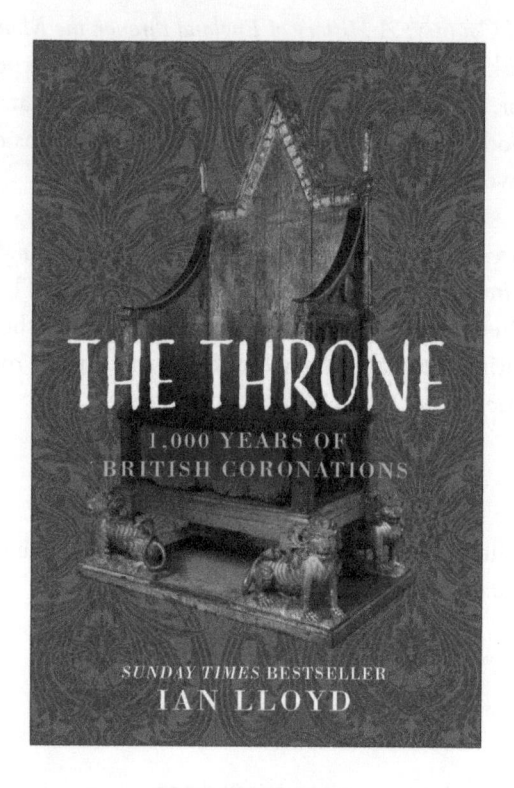

THE THRONE
1,000 YEARS OF BRITISH CORONATIONS

SUNDAY TIMES BESTSELLER
IAN LLOYD

978 1 80399 286 0

Thirty-nine coronations have been held in Westminster Abbey since the Norman Conquest: in *The Throne*, Ian Lloyd turns his inimitable, quick-witted style to these key events in British royal history, providing fascinating anecdotes and interesting facts.

The History Press
The destination for history
www.thehistorypress.co.uk